Rui Lança

GUARDIOLA —— vs —— MOURINHO

MORE THAN COACHES

Title
Guardiola vs Mourinho – More than coaches

Author
Rui Lança

Design and Paging
Vítor Duarte

Photography
Fingerhut / Shutterstock.com (Guardiola)
Pal2iyawit / Shutterstock.com (Mourinho)

Printing
Cafilesa

1st Edition
November 2016

ISBN
978-989-655-303-6

Legal Deposit
418375/16

clientes.primebooks@gmail.com
www.primebooks.pt
económico | rápido | seguro

INDEX

Victories must be shared with those helping us to climb our own Everest. In a holistic scope, what we do today has a little of those that crossed our path. Who helped us even if just planting small emotions and skills. I especially thank those that make my days better.

André and Miguel, three and a half for each.

A short briefing before getting into the pitch

There are no teams without leaders, and there are no leaders without teams. More than an organisational or sports sentence, this is the base of team work. It is one of the pieces that sustains human behaviour. And, among other pieces there are many we will try to decipher in this book, taking examples from sports, with a special focus on the actions and thoughts of two great managers, who teach us every day that, in what concerns performance, there are no recipes but behaviours that can make more of our wishes come true.

José Mourinho and Pep Guardiola are probably doing what other managers do. Probably what most of us would do. It is easier and easier to discover what each of these managers do. And we understand that the difference is not just in what they do, but mainly in how they do it. Not in the message but in the way they convey it. Not in the actions per se, but when and how they perform them.

Leadership lives with communication. In some days there are more personal interactions, in others less. Same happens with behaviours, being that quantity does not mean quality and it is up to us to understand how some leaders are more efficient in communicating, managing conflicts, managing their talent and the talent of those surrounding them. And once again what emotional intelligence is and how it works on practical cases.

All this is already too complex, but to make each day more difficult these skills, the intelligences, the actions, and the talents exist within a context of collective work. Teams composed of selfhoods, where one tool may not fit each and every one. And it is up to each group member to understand how and why some actions get better results for a specific member and not that much to others.

To your marks!

"I gave everything, there is nothing left.
And that is fundamental.
And I need to feel myself again."

Pep Guardiola (When he left Barcelona)

"Winning is the only thing that keeps you having faith in what you do"

José Mourinho

On last May 26, the gods gave us the confirmation of a long expected and desired gift! José Mourinho joins Pep Guardiola in the Premier League and, to the delight of many of us, in the same town and not 500 km apart as they were in Spain. Twelve years after his great achievement in the Champions League, the Portuguese finally signed a contract with Manchester United, in a ceremony away from the public, having just been speculated that he was wearing a tie with de Red Devils colours.

On July 5th, his first public appearance with the United colours, Mourinho made and ambitious presentation speech.

> *"I am where I want to be. I don't hide, I chase Sir Alex's record in the Champions League. I feel a bit frustrated for not being in the Champions League. Manchester United is a champions club. I want to win games, to play well, score a lot and concede little, to launch young players. I want everything. Obviously we are not going to have it all, but we want it."*

As soon as the signing of the contract was confirmed, Carlo Ancelloti referred to this moment as "a good marriage for both parties, since each needed to find such a partner".

As in astronomy, where from time to time we witness rare and magnificent events, the2016/17season will bring us similar football events. The meeting of the two coaches in Manchester and the direct and indirect confrontations between the Portuguese and the Spanish manager have everything to be an event for us to enjoy from the bench and be dazzled.

The media exposure is such that almost relegates to a second level victorious and exceptional names like Conte, Klopp, Wenger, Pochettino, Ranieri, or many others among the high level professionals working in England. Fortunately for us.

Mourinho, 8 years older than Guardiola, stated in his official presentation, that great clubs are for great managers. Clubs with a history of winnings. Thus giving the hint that the other candidates to the title might not be that great. The Portuguese has won, in his career, more than twice the games of Pep, and 23 trophies, one more than Pep.

José Mourinho and Pep Guardiola are two of the best football coaches that football and sports offered us. To benefit from the procedures and leadership results of these two experts, not only in what concerns football, but also understanding what is the relationship and harmony between the leader and the team, is a unique opportunity. May be because of this, everything they do raises a lot of curiosity and it is object of journalistic and scientific research. There is a belief that a lot of data can be taken from their lectures, training, games, actions at the substitute bench, or even from the way they react at press conferences after their victories or defeats.

The reunion comes up at different stages of their careers. Gone are the days of confrontations in Spain, but the moment does not diminish their quality. One can say that Guardiola, in cognitive terms, is closer to the stage where Mourinho was when he was in Chelsea for the first time. More pragmatic, more like a leader, leaving a bit of the manager behind and being more like an educator. But he is still more a manager than a leader and more interested in educating than in the competitive edge. However he is distancing himself from his game concept, from the collective intelligence, and the way how everyone interacts.

Having a strong base and identity, there are for sure certain improved aspects and details and others hidden in their minds during this part II paths through Munich and London. Both show an excellent mental structure, meaning that all steps are thoroughly thought of and articulated, and to watch them is a delight for those into the areas of management and team leadership.

Of course that their leadership is different! Although leadership gathers the individual characteristics of the leader, his behaviour, beliefs, and feelings, plus the situational and contextual issues, we still can find similar patterns in some managers. However equal patterns are almost impossible. In this case it is easy to say that they are quite different. In some aspects even opposed.

Mourinho and Guardiola are perfectionists. At their level there is no other way. They are focused on strictly following collective rules, so as to not be caught off guard. They are excellent communicators, but ina quite different way. We realise that, for Mourinho, being an actor is something almost intentionally authentic. The Portuguese anticipates and gets ready in a more pragmatic way. The Catalan is more natural, although his passage by Bavarian lands modified a little the way he communicates in public, having become more restrained.

In what concerns conflict management, we perceive Mourinho as being more calm, showing less anxiety and trying to capitalize on those conflicts. Pep, from what we could see on the last few years, tries to solve the conflicts by anticipating them. With their differences, without passing judgement on who is better or worse, they are two coaches presenting visible differences in their behaviour.

Some say that Mourinho shoots to the head and Guardiola to the heart.

On the other hand, these two coaches are always facing challenges in what concerns motivation and the surprise factor, since they keep raising one's expectations about what they are going that makes them stand out from all others.

Besides their technical and tactical quality, people always expect from these two something more in terms of leadership. Mourinho appeared in Italy speaking Italian at his presentation, leaving us drooling in anticipation, sensing he was getting ready for the challenge before the others. Guardiola did the same when he went to Munich. The Portuguese was on the spotlight again on the first season the second time he worked in Chelsea, but on the next one something went wrong in unusual fields. Guardiola placed his bet – as always – on tactical innovation, as a way to self-motivate and to motivate those working with him. However he wasn't able to get the cherry on top of the cake by winning the Champions League.

The Portuguese coach arrives to United after an unsuccessful and incomplete season in London. Worse than that, the season was weird, since it started immediately after him achieving the title on the Premier League, with very unusual issues on the teams and leaderships, like the Eva Carneiro case or the eclipse of some players. The Catalan, on the other hand, transfers to the City after the "guaranteed" success in Munich, without obtaining, in either season, more than the usual: to win with more or less thoroughness the national competitions.

We have to wait and see, but it seems that these two magicians got together to organise a kind of All-Stars meeting in the United Kingdom. One of these days we are going to start demanding that the best coaches as well as the best players are all in the UK.

When choosing the Portuguese coach, José Mourinho, the Manchester United used not only sports criteria, but also the values of the Red Devils organisation, which were established by Alex Ferguson. The opportunity for the Portuguese coach to claim a season (and an identity) longer than the one he managed to have in London when working in Chelsea.

On the other hand, the Catalan Pep Guardiola will want to do in England what he did in Spain and Germany: to strengthen a game culture, and a model of freedom and autonomy in his teams, in a way they are able to think, feel and decide almost by themselves. However, he knows that it is essential to win. With no victories, only a few or no one resists. His statement, after the third season in a row without placing Bayern in the finals of the Champions League, proves it:

> *"To get to the finals of the Champions was a goal. Now is up to the media to say how my performance here was. I did my work the best I could; I gave my life for this club. (...) I will be judged for not winning the Champions League."*

Both Mourinho and Guardiola could use the words of the Spanish coach when he was in Barcelona and which tell a bit of how high the competition goes at this stage:

> *"I promise we are going to work hard. I cannot say if we are going to win, but we are going to try our best. Therefore buckle up and enjoy the ride. We are going to start our journey. I am ready to grab this challenge and believe me, if I wasn't, I wouldn't be here. It is going to be a long journey but we are persistent. The team will run, and please don't worry about that. But there isn't a single player or coach that can assure success at the beginning of the season. There are no magic formulas. Even because if there were, football would no longer be interesting."*

It won't be easy for any of the managers and it is expected, opposite to what happened in Spain, that the games might be even more spiced by other clubs and Premier League opponents, like Arsenal, Liverpool, Chelsea, Tottenham and unlikely, although unfair not to mention it, Leicester or some other club like it.

This book will explain what they do and how they do it in what concerns leadership, communication, emotional management and motivation. Nowadays these two excellent managers master several areas of training and leadership, beyond the game models or systems. They dominate and enhance their behaviours, their beliefs and their feelings.

It will be interesting to watch how they are going to fit in this Premier League, being in a country that loves good practices and sports ethics, and that, on the other hand, will thrill with the combination of Guardiola and Mourinho. Probably the other managers will be left behind by the British media. The show is about to start. Take your seats and it is time to enjoy the magic!

Two Magicians way beyond Football

*"If one of my players is down,
no one will step on him; we will all
give him a hand and pull him up."*

José Mourinho

*"We cannot always be looking ourselves in the
mirror and say we are good. When things
are well is when we need to pay more
attention. The fear to lose is one of the
main reasons to play well."*

Pep Guardiola

Leadership and team sports have always been appreciated by society and organisations, and are studied within the scope of the competitiveness, commitment, union, decision taking, talent and leadership of their managers. Many cases have been studied and afterwards transposed and adapted to organisations and for the daily routine of a leader and his team.

This approach of sports to the business world has been a reality and resulted, in the mid-90s, in several analogies between sports and companies. Books on these two areas have been published as well as academic literature, where psychology and management researchers try to identify specific areas where the connection between the two domains could be performed and, for instance, analyse why company managers regularly use sports terminology, or even the similarities between elite athletes and CEOs of the Fortune 500.

Guardiola and Mourinho made it possible for many organisations to learn what happens and how some phenomena occur in other realities similar to those occurring in companies. The way the two managers, with quite different backgrounds and life experiences, are able to get their message across, and the way they make their players believe in that same message, putting into practice their ideas, is simply amazing. Many, in the business world and even in society, wish they would have that ability to get their players or subordinates to daily accomplish ideas which are better for everyone and not just for themselves.

Good practices of leadership, team management, decision making, competitiveness, and self-organisation within the reality and organisational context where Mourinho and Guardiola work, are always a good opportunity, both for the common citizen and the leaders of big companies, to get good examples, always keeping in mind to adapt to and contextualise within the different realities where they perform their activities.

Another amazing angle of this synergy between Mourinho and Guardiola and the leadership is that these two magicians of training and leadership make us talk about the leadership they transmit to their players; the leadership they delegate on and share with their teams, although not with all the athletes in the same way. Talking about leadership no longer means talking about the manager in this specific field.

Leadership may include the coaches, captains and other athletes in whom the managers see the skills for the job. It is the role of the managers to evaluate and improve their capacities. It is also the role of José Mourinho and Pep Guardiola to know how to relate with their athletes, as was for instance the case of Lahm or Lampard, and make them the leaders on the pitch.

Imagine yourself working with someone really talented, or even someone that common sense would define as having potential. That person wouldn't or shouldn't be treated like the others. If we treat everyone the same way we won't be able for sure to get the best of each. Mind that treating people differently does not mean discrimination against or unequal treatment. Dealing with people in different ways will make them give the best they have. It is the job of each of us to understand what we can do to trigger the best in others and make them operate at their best.

The volleyball coach, Júlio Velasco, gave the following advice to Pep Guardiola when he was starting is career and seeing Leonel Messi as talented player but also as a challenge, knowing he would have to profit from all the skills of the football star:

> "You will have to know how to seduce him, engage to get the best of him. Your job is all about that and we all need it because we all depend on each other."

To be a coach and a leader in sports includes technical skills that will improve the performance of the athletes; the capacity to influence the psychological development and well-being of the athletes; understanding the important role played in making the athlete get down to business; and also give the athlete more control and freedom for him to carry out the actions devised by the coach and needed by the team to accomplish the common goals.

And how is it like to be what many wish? Is it something that could be transferred to other sciences? These are two of Pep Guardiola's visions that will make us understand his vision and the rhetoric of his job:

> "To be a coach is being under pressure. Coaches are alone, no one is with us. We are with four people of our staff who won't to follow us and the players we convince to be with us. Coaches are more alone than anyone."[1]

> "Being a coach is fascinating. And this is why it is so difficult to quit. It is so sweet, a steady feeling of excitement, your brain doesn't stop."[2]

---

[1] Perarnau, M. (2014)
[2] Balague, G. (2012)

Besides all the technical and tactical knowledge, or the physical capacities for the game and of the athletes in general, the managers must also master interpersonal skills, like emotional intelligence, ability to motivate and inspire, manage conflicts, and also the ability to align all the members of the team to reach the common goal. It is not easy and any of us could go crazy with so much information and the need to manage such different fields.[3]

The role of the coach as a leader within sports is becoming more and more valued and researched, due to its importance for the success (or failure) of his athletes. The technical skills focus on the ability to support and motivate the athletes to be aware of their strengths and of their personal limit in order to offer the best performance. If we think carefully, the coaches could teach some company managers how it is done.

Guardiola e Mourinho are assumed as perfect examples of coaching for the multinational companies operating in Spain and Portugal. The type of "coach" who gets the maximum performance from his workers and improves self-confidence. Sometimes we are not talking about powerful and refined leadership techniques. We talk about simple gestures. We talk about the foundations of interpersonal relationships, about the foundations of team management and leadership.

When Guardiola was still manager at Barcelona B and, at the same time, father of his third child, with all that turmoil of emotions, he visited the Argentinian defender, Gabriel Milito at the Quirón Hospital. The defender had had surgery on his right knee and was surprised with the visit of the Catalan coach. They talked for 3 hours about Argentinian football.

One of the many goals of a manager is to be able to develop skills in his athletes and teams, aiming to obtain better decisions and making them act for longer in an autonomous or in a freer way, without losing quality of performance. And also, within this scope,

[3] Lança, R. & Lopes, M.P. (2015)

both coaches are masters in how quick they impose their way of working and of being, taking into account the cultures and characteristics of the players in their teams.

The goalkeepers' coach of Barcelona, Juan Carlos Unzué, lost his father to a long-term disease in 2008. With a match scheduled for the next day in Malaga, Guardiola took the whole team to the small town of Orkoien in Navarre, 800 km from Malaga, to attend the funeral. On the next day, Barcelona won the match. A score of 4 to 1, but numbers in this case don't really matter.

Another reclaimed and acclaimed skill of top leaders is empathy. The ability to get into another person's shoes, developing emotional intelligence due to understanding the emotions and feelings of others. A story that truly tells this skill is the invitation that Guardiola made to Cristóbal, who had no education or work, and was living on the help of Barcelona´s managers, coaches and players who crossed his path in Camp Nou. The Barcelona's coach decided to invite him to have lunch every day at the Club's canteen, together with all the players and thus being able to witness another reality, side by side with his heroes.

These are the skills and human capacity, together with the perfect management of people that call the attention of institutions and companies worldwide. Mourinho, Guardiola, Wayne Smith, Mike Kryzewski and other renowned managers are regularly contacted to go to top companies and pass on their knowledge and beliefs about business "locker rooms" management. Even because both in the sports and the business worlds, the members of the team show a high level of alignment in what they perceive as the leader's behaviour, suggesting a high degree of consistency in the evaluation of that same behaviour.

The nature of the environment where sports and business teams work has, however, changed and as a consequence new needs came up, and research and practices don't always adapt to the emerging needs. Presently, most of the sports teams work in a more dynamic, demanding and complex environment than they did in the past. Environments that change and adapt in a more regular way and work with more flexible boundaries.

It is not easy to find in the same person all the characteristics that José Mourinho and Pep Guardiola gather. These two managers and leaders show high levels of emotional intelligence, controlling their emotions and anticipating those of others, almost envisioning what each of their actions is going to cause.

Neither is it easy to find players that have been coached by both. Xabi Alonso worked with both of them and in a less expansive way kept saying that he considered both coaches very similar in the way they worked and how demanding they were.

Zlatan Ibrahimovic, ex-star of PSG and who played for Barcelona in 2009/10, coached by Guardiola, has no problem assuming his preference for the Portuguese coach. The striker wanted to join the Real Madrid, coached at the time by Mourinho. And all because he didn't get along with Pep and wanted to work again with José Mourinho, after the two having been together in Inter (2008/09). The Swedish made the disclosure in his autobiography, where he was not soft when referring to the Catalan:

> "*I was lost and expected Guardiola to say something, but he is a coward. He made me a worse player. He didn't even say "good morning". Not a single word. He avoided looking me in the eyes. If I entered a room, he would leave. "What is happening?" I thought. "Is it something I said? Did I look or spoken something wrong?" All those things got inside my head in a bad way and I couldn't get any sleep. I constantly thought about him and this".*

On Mourinho, the speech was smoother:

> *Mourinho would turn you into a kid who basically would die for him. Works the double than the rest, lives and breathes football 24 hours a day, seven days a week. I never met a coach with knowledge of the two sides. He was everywhere. Mourinho build personal bonds with the players with his text messages and knowledge about our situation with wives and children. He would cheer us up before the matches, it was like a theatre, a psychological game."*

The Swedish ends up fulfilling his dream and joins José Mourinho in Manchester to help the Portuguese return to the victories on British lands.

Pep and José show self-confidence; self-management capacity; adaptability to new contexts and situations; are highly competitive; show initiative to innovate; empathy with their athletes; organisational skills; intuition; influence; ability to delegate their leadership on the field; ability to deal with the human side of people; they do not criticize their own in public, and know how to manage conflicts. And these are the most important characteristics of a leader in any field we might be focusing.

António Damásio[4], director of the Brain and Creativity Institute, University of Southern California, assumes that, for him, the most interesting thing about the Mourinho phenomenon (and probably Guardiola would fit in too) has nothing to do specifically with football:

> "It concerns each and every sports team, but also companies, orchestras or political parties. It has to do with the way several performers behave around a single project, as they were a single entity, although keeping their own individualities."

He proceeds, mentioning the leadership qualities:

> "Leadership quality, among which the ability to conceive an action plan and transmitting the image of that project to a group of performers, in a not only clear, but also motivating way. The high quality leaders imagine the project, both the big picture and the details of its organisation and the possible variations to its development. (...) The process requires to inspire a belief, a will, specially this last one – the will to achieve the best result the project could have. One of the secrets of this inspiration is to build a narrative that gives the project a meaning transcending victories or defeats, a script which stimulates yearning."

---

[4] Amieiro, N.; Barreto, R.; Oliveira, B. & Resende, N. (2006)

In sports there are no recipes for a good individual or collective performance. There are no 100% correct formulas for a manager to act and assume the leadership and the training of his athletes, groups, and teams. There are, in fact, behaviours and attitudes that are in general associated to more successful results. Whatever success means!

We know that a team needs a leader. And that it has to work according to its best resource: the whole. But we also know that there are no managers or leaders without teams! It is essential that the manager is able to improve all his knowledge and skills.

Managers are always looking to increase their knowledge and to use it as a way to accomplish their goals. Nowadays this is the only way to survive. They also practice to improve their technical, tactical, and physical knowledge. Mourinho talking at the launch of a course at his former university in Portugal stated exactly this: "It is no longer about the quantity of knowledge you have but what you do with it."

Hence the need to potentiate and perceive how each manager works and how he profits from everything it happens to him and from what surrounds him. The New Zealander rugby coach Wayne Smith talked at a training session in Oxford about his transition from player to manager and the daily learning process which needs to be one of the main focuses of any coach:

> "*I get the necessary skills from the management world and with managers. They educated me. They made me wish to daily demand more from myself so I can improve. They taught me to develop a constant approach to develop a project or improve a team. I learned that the process of a team needs constant goals which need to be analysed. I read a lot about training, coaching and management books. They complete me and add to the traditional values of rugby, give us a better vision and a path to always want to be better. I like to learn with the past but I don't live there.*"

To better understand the scope of a manager and of leadership, we give you the definition of football coach by Professor Manuel Sérgio, who was very important in José Mourinho's career path:

"Only those who know more than football know football; only those knowing more than sports know sports. It is not enough to just know what specifically concerns football to be a good football coach. The coach must know about football, must have practiced football, because those who don't practice don't know. You only true know what you experience. Theory is not enough. Assuming that the coach knows what football is what distinguishes the good ones from the less good?The human qualities. Because we are in the human area."[5]

On the other hand, the coach that Guardiola replaced in Bayern Munich, Jupp Heynckes, has a peculiar approach to leadership and human resources management:

"The specialists of each area are probably much better than me in that specific context. I think, however, that the main coach must have a clear notion of what the team/players need to train, not only within the technical and tactical plan but also physically and psychologically. Once I give my opinion, it is up to the specialist to prepare the exercise. Of course this process must be consensual and always starts with a dialogue and exchange of ideas among the members of the technical team. We work together and the success of the team is primarily of the players and then of the technical team, not of myself."[6]

There is a big focus on José and Pep and, on the way, they are able to engage their teams, keep them together and working independently in order to defeat their opponents. And it is here that these two managers can be great role models, being more than two excellent managers. They can be a good lesson for working teams, leaving three topics: how to motivate the team; how to organize the team; and how to make it work.

Nothing like quoting John Wooden, considered to be the best coach of NCAA ever, with his ten champion cups – American college basketball and we remind the media coverage of college basketball in the USA, as a school for the best sport coaches of

---

[5] *Sérgio, M. (2009)*
[6] *Lança, R. (2014)*

collective sports of the world. He is known for a series of quotes that have become beliefs for many coaches. The need for the coach to understand that talent is quite important but not enough, was one of his biggest fights. Wooden states that skill takes us to the top, but that character is needed to keep us there: "To win once you need talent, to win again takes character."

José Mourinho

José Mário dos Santos Mourinho Félix, Setúbal, 53 years old, 26 of January, 1963. Elected in 2011 as best coach for FIFA based on his performance in 2010.

He starts his career in 2000, working in Benfica with a defeat of 1-0 against Boavista. Although he hasn't coached in many clubs, he stood out in most of them: FC Porto, Chelsea, Inter Milan and, why not, Real Madrid.

In spite of several victories in all the clubs he coached, the most significant are the victories in Champions League when working for FC Porto and Inter Milan, in 2003/04 and 2009/10, respectively.

Key strengths: Mourinho has always been known by his exceptional communication skills, commitment to the athletes and those mind games or skill to anticipate and see the obvious before the others. He is a staunch defender of his people.

Points to improve: One of the risks of a leadership like that of Mourinho is that you cannot remain indifferent, either you love him and are with him or you get worn out by the intensity. The strain of a winning season in Chelsea turning into one where almost everything was lost is for sure a proof of the intensity and lack of ability to answer to new situations.

Collective processes: Like almost all top coaches, Mourinho lives for his missions. He likes to decorate and prepare in detail the interactions with the players and to improve a strong cohesion of the team, which is shown by the defensive behaviour of the team and the way the players take his side.

Leadership: If we had to point out a style or a profile, José Mourinho could be described as a manager focused in training (continuous improvement) and a mix of management and relationship, taking into account his implicit and almost unique need of being in a team that is with him, his values, and ideals.

Communication: Mourinho was one of the first coaches, in this era of news to the minute, that new how to potentiate all his communication moments, when his messages weren't intended for who asked but for those listen somewhere. He almost always gets a communicational impact and manages that his message is shared by his best messengers, the athletes.

My name is Mourinho, José Mourinho. This could well be the introduction of José Mourinho. May be in his own opinion, it should be James Bond to ask some kind of permission to the Portuguese to use some of the best sentences of the coach born in Setúbal. Mourinho is also this, a person, a manager, and a leader with an incredible self-confidence.

José Mourinho works hard on his image, even though almost in a genuine way! He knows how important it is to manage well what he says, all the communication channels and how far his words reach. If there are researches that state that those leading are also story tellers, tellers of ideas, of a vision, of a gratifying and demanding challenge, than Mourinho is an excellent story teller! We stay for days thinking about his words.

Alex Ferguson, for instance, assumes in his autobiography that is first impression when Mourinho arrived to England was "What as... young prude", but he had the notion that he was going to be the new kid on the block. Young, but better not to argue with him since he seemed to have intelligence and trust enough to fight."He is one of those young men that stay on the surf board longer than the others". The first altercation with Mourinho was during the match FC Porto eliminated United from the Champions League with a goal of Costinha near the end of the match.

The assistant of the Scottish, the Portuguese Carlos Queiroz, had warned them in advance: "He is a very intelligent lad: "He was by far my best student." José Mourinho had studied with Alex Ferguson's assistant in Portugal.

But first things first. Beginning of the match or, in this case, of Mourinho's career. And the truth is his story would make an Oscar nomination movie. Undoubtedly. Possibly even with Mourinho playing as himself. And one of the most outstanding scenes is when Bobby Robson left FC Porto to go to Barcelona and specifically asked that Mourinho went with him. At the time, the issue of being or not a translator put the Portuguese on everyone's lips.

He already stated that he has never been a translator, but the former President of Barcelona, Joan Gaspart, assures that he was accepted in Camp Nou as such. This happened back in 1996 when Robson, bi-champion in FC Porto, moved to Barcelona, hired by the president of the club at the time, Josep Lluis Nunez:

> "The day we signed the contract, Mr. Nunez had a small discussion with Robson, because he didn't want to hire a translator. Robson told him it was very important. Nunez agreed and offered Mourinho 10 thousand pesetas a month. Mourinho said that he could not live with the amount Barça was paying him."

Mourinho complained that with 10 thousand pesetas (around 60 euros) he could not make a living. "He lived for the first months in one of my hotels for free, because he had no Money. But when he showed that he was much more than a translator, Barcelona gave him a raise. In the end, Mr. Nunez accepted to increase the payment, but not much."disclosed Joan Gaspart.

He had the following opinion about Mourinho: "Alone he was a charming person, but he has a split personality", Gaspar stated. That's not such a big surprise since José Mourinho himself publically admitted that he doesn't like to see himself as a manager, not seeing himself mirrored in his attitudes, hence the need to be an actor sometimes.

The players tell several episodes where his words and interventions left a mark on them. Even players that José kept more time on the bench than playing, like the Italian Materazzi who assumed that "that hug was the end of two great years, he was a part of a family, he was the leader of a family who was willing to face everything and all.", talking about the time Mourinho left Inter and a camera captured Mourinho getting out of his vehicle and giving a warm hug to the defender.

Another athlete, the Swedish Ibrahimovic, who worked with Mourinho in Italy and before he was confirmed as a player of the Reds, considered that the club of Manchester had made a good decision in contracting Mourinho:

> "If you want action you get Mourinho. I believe he is the man who is going to bring them to the top again. Where ever he was, he won. He knows what he is doing. If you want to win get Mourinho. I liked very much the time I worked with him. When I left Inter I told him: 'We had little time together, but it was very good." On the same interview, the Swedish confided that he spoke daily with Mourinho even because "it is no secret that I have a good relationship with him and we always keep in touch".

But are there also players that might have other stories to tell about the Portuguese coach relating to not so good issues or events? Of course, but we will find that with both Mourinho and Guardiola. The focus is to understand why there are so many players who worked with the Portuguese manager and even when they didn't play, they still adored him! Another not very known fact about Mourinho is that, like Guardiola, he also searches in other sports information about how he can learn and transpose to football, like for instance in the NBA.

Besides being a good story teller, Mourinho sometimes has a good sense of humour. Not much of a British humour, but now and then he was able to get some laughs from the reporters. Here is one statement that translates his sense of humour and tries to mix a bit of humbleness but a lot of confidence: "If they made a movie about my life, they should get George Clooney to do my role." And his playful side comes out again when he continues "he's an amazing actor and my wife thinks he would be perfect."

On the other hand he acts as someone who leads quite well with opposing behaviours, without losing sight of one of his main focus: that the message reaches the people in front of him, but also the collateral effects the message might have on other receivers. A good example of his ability to assume several roles, as a top actor, is the management of some of his assistants.

As José stated, "I had so many assistants in my career", what may show that, on one hand, the Portuguese manager chooses his assistants well, even because some of them followed their careers as main coaches with good results, or, on the other hand, that his intense and demanding personal interaction ends up being stressful (not everyone keeps up with him) leaving wounded in this battle for team leadership within a highly competitive environment.

Talking about André Villas-Boas, one of his assistants who left in a quite turbulent way the technical team when Mourinho was at the Inter, Mourinho stated that he would drink a glass of wine with him, even "because when people invite me I always go, I never say no".

In 2010, at the Awards ceremony of the Business Journalists Association, the President of Real Madrid, Florentino Pérez, let slip that Mourinho was paid fifteen million Euros each season. He immediately tried to excuse himself, clarifying that it were fifteen million before taxes!

José Mourinho practiced (it is not known what will happen in Manchester) what is called the "Capello Doctrine", which sustains that the manager must earn more than any of the players in the squad. The Italian manager, Fabio Capello, earned in Real Madrid one Euro more than the most expensive player, and as Britain's national manager the total amount of nine million Euros. Vicente del Bosque, for instance, who was world champion with the Spanish National Team, earned slightly above two million.

José Mourinho is, in general, one of the best paid managers. Ironically when his salaries were discussed in Spain, someone reminded that when he came the first time to Spain he was earning sixty euros a month!

The Portuguese manager never had a problem in recurring to his history to answer some jealous comments, as it happened when he was hired by Real Madrid and his not very positive relationship particularly with Madrid's media, but also with the Spanish media in general. He even stated:

> "I think Real Madrid cannot have a coach without achievements. Now they have a coach with two victories in Champions, six tournaments in different countries, with cups, 17 titles, and even so, it raises so many doubts, that if a poor coach with no titles arrives here, no matter how good, how phenomenal he is, they will kill him."

He can be as human as it gets when he goes to poorer countries promoting humanitarian campaigns or he can show an ego the size of the world. A committed catholic, he considers that "God must really think I am a fantastic lad, otherwise he wouldn't have given me so much." But on the other hand he never goes unnoticed and therefore the football fans either love him or reject him. The mythical Johan Cruyff even stated: "I have a lot of respect for Mourinho as a coach, but he will never be the coach of my team".

Looking at Mourinho's career, although he has had amazing performances in Chelsea and a less glamorous in Madrid, it is in the cities of Milan and Oporto, in Inter and FC Porto, respectively, that his sports seasons reach their peak, with four years full of titles and all the players admiring him..

The mythical captain Zanetti talked about the importance of having had Mourinho as coach: "we exchanged a few strong words, coming from the heart, both sincere; we were able to build a great friendship". Costinha, who score the goal, curiously against the Manchester United, that allowed FC Porto to get to the next round, shared what Mourinho said to his players: "If one of my players is down, no one will step on him; we will all give him a hand and pull him up."

All those who get to the stage reached by these two managers don't get there by chance or due to life events. They get there because they work hard and well!Vítor Baía said the following about Mourinho:

> "He is a workaholic. He just doesn't work 24 hours a day because he has his family and needs to sleep, otherwise he would do it. Therefore, except for sleeping and family, he is always working, programming and anticipating, programming and anticipating... And the players can clearly feel the passion he has for what he does."[7]

From all the clubs he worked, Real Madrid was the hardest horse to tame. But he did it. He ended up leaving without winning the Champions League, but with the assumed belief he had imposed is values, contrary to what was said that it would be the club taming him. Valdano, at the time the director of the Madrid club, assumed that it would be the club to tame the Portuguese:

> "Mourinho? Mourinho decided to replace Real Madrid's values by his own, in order to build an army against Barça. He is a coach with quite a strong personality, especially if the club lets him. It is true that there was a short circuit between us. The interaction between us became impossible and Florentino chose Mourinho."

It is difficult to please everyone. And this is not what the manager wants! He wants to be able to keep all his players satisfied and

---

[7] Lourenço, L. (2010)

committed to the challenges, both personal and collective, it is a challenge and a remarkable feat. Sometimes defining goals is an undervalued task. And within this scope, Mourinho knows exactly how to make each athlete define their own goals. The Everest that the athlete will want to climb. Not only for his own pleasure when reaching the top, but because he allowed the team to reach the top too. Metaphorically speaking, the mountain doesn't have to be the same for everyone. It has to be demanding, challenging, bonding, consistent, motivating, and to always allow the development of personal and team skills.

Pep Guardiola

Josep Guardiola i Sala, Santpedor, 45 years old, 18 of January, 1971. He became the best new coach of all times when he got the title in the Spanish Championship, the King's Cup, the Spain's Super Cup, UEFA's Champions League, European Super Cup, and the Club World Cup. Adding to that he also got several awards as best coach of the year.

He formally starts his career taking the reins at Barcelona B on June 21st 2007. He was champion of the Spanish third division. On May 8th 2008, Guardiola was officially nominated Barcelona's manager, leaving afterwards to Munich, with a one year gap in the middle.

Guardiola had a dazzling beginning, having wan his best titles on those first seasons. At Bayer Munich, he won everything at national level, but he didn't get the Champions League for the Bavarian club.

Key Strengths: Guardiola is passionate and transmits that captivating passion. Although not as strongly, he still is quite spontaneous and with a leadership based on transformational and visionary actions.

Points to improve: He was confronted with internal issues of the Munich club that got him exposed to less football related fields or in fields that a less binding management didn't find a solution for those actions. He was left hanging in what concerns the true impact of those actions.

Collective processes: At this level one can only emphasise the collective over the individual. Even working with several stars, he was always able to put the collective first, hence his leadership based on alignment, meritocracy, open communication and even getting some stars out of his squad.

Leadership: He is a manager with a more training and coaching approach, investing in the delegation of responsibilities, and game and behaviour empowerment. A clear and positive speech, that always focus on his players being those contributing to reach the goals of the team.

Communication: Straightforward, authentic, and appealing to emotional values. Not very imperative or conflicting, but being nevertheless assertive. The German environment and the experience gained over the years made him more pragmatic and careful with the words.

Guardiola. Pep Guardiola. Half intellectual, half left wing, likes poetry. Catalan and supporter of Catalonia's independence. He answers the questions asked in English or German in the same language. When questioned in Spanish, he usually answers in Catalan. Son of a mason of Santpedor, in Catalonia, assumes that one of the main lessons he learned with his father was to learn how to lose, never blaming others.

The Italian manager, Fabio Capello, while still manager of the British national team, stated on the intellectuality of the Catalan:

> *"He is one of the few intellectuals I had the pleasure to meet. Intellectual in the sense that he thinks about a lot of things. A lot about football, of course, but also about literature and other cultural issues".*

Pep loves to read and travel. The coach states that when he starts the project of a new journey, he tries to collect knowledge for his work in different areas of management. He can be listening to people for hours and after that get the best of each briefing. Among the several managers he listened to during his journey as a coach, he pointed out names like Johan Cruyff, Cesar Luis Menotti, Juan Manuel Lillo, Marcelo Bielsa, and Arrigo Sacchi.

When he was living in Italy, he travelled several kilometres to meet the Argentinian volleyball coach, Julio Velasco, in person, just because he had watched an interview of the Argentinian on television and really wanted to learn with him. In a normal conversation, Guardiola generally has more questions than answers. Regardless of the media attention he gets, Guardiola asks questions after questions, with the curiosity of a child.

Pep was just 37 years old when he won his first Champions League, becoming the youngest manager ever to win this trophy. But it wasn't only as a manager that Pep became famous in Catalonia. As player he won 17 trophies, including six national titles and the gold medal at the Olympics. As Barcelona's manager he just wasn't able to win against one of his opponents: Chelsea. He lost the four matches against them.

He has earned a lot of money in his carrier, not only as a coach, but also as a player. When he signed the contract to coach the main team of Barcelona, Guardiola was going to occupy the office of his predecessor, the Dutch Frank Rijkaard. As he spent countless hours in that space, the Catalan bought a plasma TV to analyse the matches of his team and of his opponents, the most curious being that he paid it from his own pocket.

Guardiola, like Mourinho, is obsessed with details. The midfielder Xavi says the same:

> "He never gives us a minute's rest. He's like a dog with a bone, football is everything to him and he is very intense in all he does. We could say he is almost obsessed with football."

And winning games is all in the details, stated Crujff. Many consider that Guardiola in Barcelona did the best football ever, together with titles. For someone inexperienced as manager, coming from a football player career, full of successes and praises, Pep managed to build a team that surpassed the opponent when keeping hold of the ball, and amazingly, even when they didn't, which didn't happen often taking the percentages of ball possession presented by Barcelona.

Besides the level of rigour, Guardiola always reiterated his passion for everything he does. It was the only way to get what he set as goal since he was a player: to be an excellent manager and that he would bring that to every club he went. When he signed with Bayern he stated:

> *"I love football. I started to like it even before I started to play it. And I still like to play. I love to watch, I love to speak about football. I am going to lock myself in that room and try to learn as much as possible about the club, and as fast as possible."*

On the other hand, passion makes the pragmatic Catalan say something like this:

> *"The day I understand that light and magic are no longer in the eyes of my players, it is time for me to leave."*

In Munich he tried something similar, but he missed the cherry on top of the cake. A title in the Champions League. Taking into account the excellent players and the team spirit he managed to get in Germany, he possibly missed a Messi. The Dutch striker, Bergkamp, stated something that was not often brought to public discussion, during a final where the Italian team from Torino almost knocked out Guardiola's squad: "Is Bayern individually that good that it would be a shame to be knocked out by Juventus? It only seems like they are, because the way they play makes them look much better than they are", pointing out the excellent work and improvement of some players, achieved by the Catalan coach during the years he was in Munich.

Vítor Pereira, ex-manager and champion of FC Porto, worked for a couple of days with Guardiola in Munich. During a conversation with the Catalan, the Portuguese Vítor Pereira asked him about working on some tactical aspects with other exercises to obtain, in the opinion of the former coach of FC Porto, more efficient results. He tells that the next day the assistant coach, Manuel Estiarte, asks him the following question: "What did you give to Pep? He spent the whole afternoon locked in his office, it looked like someone gave him a new toy..."

To define Pep Guardiola is not an easy task. There are no perfect professionals in any profession, but the Catalan has been reaching new heights in many of the tasks and roles of a manager. And, sooner or later, everyone is tested and, in time, there are always areas that can be improved. But every top manager, Guardiola, Mourinho, or other, test themselves before they test others.

This is one of the most valued common denominators of demanding and winning managers: their self-determination in always focusing first more on themselves than on others. Not in a selfish or self-centred way, but because it is a part of their level of demand and ability to always want to be the best at what they do. This way they are better prepared to manage and coach the other group of experts, the players.

The Catalan journalist, Marti Peramau, author of the book "Herr Pep", stated that Guardiola "is a man who has doubts about everything" and that they come up not due to mistrust or fear but because it is "a part of his search for perfection". It is only normal that Guardiola, like is future rival of Manchester United, captivate all the people who love the phenomenon of football and leadership of people and teams. In his première as main coach, Pep managed with his Barcelona to win all that was to be wan.

Although having formally started his career as manager of Barça B, it was in Mexico that the Catalan gave his first steps as coach of the Dorados, highly influenced by the admiration of manager Juanma Lillo. The Mexican claims that he always considered

Guardiola to have everything to become a good manager, since "he analysed everything with the mind of a manager, not only as a player."

Jordi Cruyff, son of the mythical Dutch player, stated that "Guardiola improved my father's aggressive game, and the pressure without ball, recover the ball as soon as possible to get it back in good circulation." A follow-up on a new way to see the football started by his father.

At the beginning of Mourinho's career we could perceive that he worked on the contents of the message and the way it was transmitted, which still happens today. As for Pep Guardiola, at the beginning of his career as manager he was much more spontaneous than when he was in Bayern Munich. This is due to the internal conflicts he had to face with Bavarian sports leaders, and today Guardiola is less spontaneous and we can perceive many answers have been previously prepared.

However, he didn't lose some of his best characteristics, to be straightforward and at the same time ironic, which is usually associated with high rates of emotional intelligence: "I am like a woman, I am able to think on more than one thing at the same time." On the other hand, Guardiola relies a lot in his passion and ability to make his players play according to his ideas. He claims that the important thing is the process, and that if he manages to apply it in an effective way he will be closer to victory: "What is important is what you do to try to win, it is the process that matters, it is the work you had so you could be able to win."

Guardiola is a man of convictions. Those who follow him may start collecting beliefs and mythical sentences to write a book. One of the key moments in Guardiola's career was a home defeat in the match Bayern Munich-Real Madrid by 0 to 4. He admitted that: "In this type of defeats you only get out in two ways, either you weaken or you rise stronger. I rise with more energy and conviction."

The seven times Guardiola competed in the Champions League he reached the semi-finals seven times. He didn't win all! Not even half of them! Because of this Guardiola might be remembered as someone who failed «at the final moments of the European competitions, although he has wan many titles, both in Spain and in Germany. Guardiola is probably recognised by his contribution to football, either you like it or not. By having created a legion of fans. And we will see if the Catalan manager will be able to regenerate himself, even because he always upheld his process and, sometimes, when it was essential to show results, he didn't make it!

One of the most fascinating characteristics of the Catalan, and not very common in these levels of demand and performance, is that during his work in Munich, one of the assistants had nothing to do with football, but yet with water polo. Manel Estiarte is known as the "Maradona of Water Polo" and he was his assistant in the German club.

Pep has this opinion about his assistant: "Managing a football team is a lonely job and that is why I value the loyalty of the technical team above all else. Manel helps me both in the training and with the happiness he shows at work and that is important in this context." Manel's experience is important and ends up helping some of the players and giving them those benefits, even because his attitude also protects Pep Guardiola a lot.

One day Guardiola was giving a talk about penalties and who would or wouldn't shoot. At certain point one of the Bavarian players asked a question and Guardiola stated that he didn't know how to take a penalty himself. He wasn't an expert. But he immediately stated: "But you have here the best penalty taker of the world." And he pointed at Estiarte: "I am talking about Manel. He was the best water polo player in the world. He took penalties better than anyone. Only four out of every five penalty kicks hit the target, but Manel put them all away!"

Guardiola has plenty of these "exceptions". Besides having an assistant coming from water polo, the Catalan absorbs many other sports. He said about his Barça that they had started to play a little more like in basketball:

> "They moved more, taking possession of the ball and moving it around the field, and changing the game rhythm. It would make them feel they had the ball for five hours when they really only were playing for 90 minutes."

Pep also wrote a book, 'La meva gente, el meu futbol', i.e.'My people, my football". This book, written in Catalan, has sold out and had the collaboration of Lu Martin and Miguel Rico, two of the most respected Spanish journalists.

In Spain, after his first year as manager of the main team of FC Barcelona, a research work on Guardiola's leadership methods became a best-seller in Spain: 'Liderazgo Guardiola'. A book detailing the key aspects to create admiration towards the manager, the team and the organisation:[8]

1. To clearly define their mission (what we are dedicated to), the vision (what we want to achieve), and the values (we consider more important)
- Besides the passion feeling the former player showed since his youth at the club, he surprised everyone with his ability to define priorities and strategy. Quoting the philosopher Daniel Inneratiy: "It is not the urgency that prevents us from making a long term project, but the absence of a project that refers us to the tyranny of the present."

2. Reputation, success attracts success.
- Pep Guardiola coached a team that besides the football they played, for many the best football ever, had other messages, like social responsibility translated in the UNICEF shirts they wore. That brought responsibility to his players and was another pillar of commitment towards what the team and the players had to produce.

---

[8] *Cubeiro, J. C. (2010).*

3. Incorporate the talent they want and need.
- Guardiola knew precisely how his team played and what type of players he needed to fill the gaps. He always had that advantage when including new players and knowing what type of profile was essential so that no gaps existed (although they existed with some layers like Etoo or Ibra).

4. Promote internal merit.
- One of the differentiating factors of the best teams and companies is the ability they have to potentiate internal resources. Promotes identity, inclusion and alignment. FC Barcelona does it like few and it does it well. It creates ambition internally and gives motivation and direction to those who feel the club from an early stage.

5. Improve the collective environment through personal leadership
- Guardiola is called a leading manager. He likes inclusion, to promote a good work environment, managing his emotions for the suitable environment according to future challenges. And he assumes that work must also be highly individualised so that it generates a satisfaction environment through everyone's performance.

6. Management of professional performance
- Advocate that motivation and the consequences of the athletes' actions plays an important role in the financial retribution that each athlete gets.

Other authors[9] take the letters of the Catalan's name and leave us a few clues:

- Gain
- Union
- Audacity
- Rigor
- Distraction

---

[9] *Cubeiro, J. C. & Galalrdo, L. (2011)*

- Innovation
- Optimism
- Leadership
- Humbleness
- Admiration

And leave other relevant clues.

- The unbreakable commitment and fidelity to a game style and identity
- The whole above the individual, union and solidarity
- Discipline and strict compliance with the rules
- Trust in those of value, no matter their age
- Tactical culture with flexibility
- Detailed and demanding when studying each opponent
- Persistence at work with dedication and effort
- Insistently self-demanding
- Group culture
- Humbleness, encouragement, enthusiasm and respect for the rival

Oliver Khan, former goalkeeper of the Bavarian, had a less positive opinion about Guardiola: "always a bit anxious and that is part of his personality." And that carried some weight in the fact that "he was always so cautious". The former German captain even stated that "it's because of it that he is always talking. Always needing to justify himself."

With a four month notice that he was going to leave Munich, Lothar Matthaus also criticized Pep. For the former captain of the Bavarian:

> "There never was love and care between Pep and the players. Those sentences of "super, super", the taps on the back and the hugs were just for the show, as well as his overreactions on the bench".

In fact, leadership has, besides all challenges and difficulties, the (in)capacity to please all. Not about the more difficult issue of everyone getting to play, but in what concerns behaviours, since the athletes also have their preferences. When Guardiola's teams win, the players are the winners, since the manager always praises that.

And the stars – excellent players – who didn't abide to his rules or didn't fit his competitive logic and group alignment – were sooner or later set aside, like Ronaldinho, Deco, Eto'o and the Swedish Ibra! When the number 10 of the Brazilian selection was set aside, Pep had a short conversation with Ronaldinho stating that it wasn't an easy decision, but that he didn't believe on the recovery of his fitness and the way the Brazilian star was dedicated to training, so he would have to search for another place to shine.

The Leadership

*"The worst defeat is when you go home feeling that you
didn't give it all, that you didn't give your best. Today
I don't have that feeling... During the break I told to
the players: You deserve to be at the finals, fight for it...
There was no tactical change, everything was OK.
But Atletico deserves to be in the finals too."*

Pep Guardiola

*"Authority fades with time and the empathy created.
A person arrives and shows who he is and what he can do,
asserts himself and establishes rules. Everyone should
feel leadership and no one should see it"*

José Mourinho

Nowadays, to speak about leadership is speaking about one of the sexiest and most captivating themes of our society. The way leadership relates to leaders, contexts, results and processes, styles and profiles, tools and methods. The media attention attained by José Mourinho and Pep Guardiola was so intense that all their quotes and interventions are a target for interpretation. One more real than others, the truth is that the attention their words and actions get, especially when directed to their players and competitors, should limit not only the contents of their interventions, but also the way they do it, where and when they do it.

On the other hand. Managers like these two experts, coach mostly competent, demanding athletes with high personal goals, within highly competitive environments and where mistakes are seldom allowed. A lot of emotional and motivational expertise is also required, since several studies show that mentally strong athletes are preferred by leaders who aim to develop the athletes' skills and improve their performance.

When investigating leadership we find, almost monthly, a set of new knowledge which results from lots of works and experiences, carried out in the sports world, with coaches, athletes, managers, structures, and teams. And this vision focuses on an important point: the need to create a relationship between the leader's vision of the goals and the leader's connection with the athletes. It requires an understanding and respect for the dynamics between those o influence and those who are influenced.

The behaviour of managers has been described by many experts working in behavioural areas like being the main link to the positive or less positive impact that the manager is able to create on the athlete and the team. His interpersonal style, the way he communicates, all this influences positively – or negatively – his athletes. To approach the leadership theme is to approach much of its behaviours and small actions that may have essential impact and return on winning or facing the opponent.

There are several ways to climb a mountain. How to climb it, it is the choice of just one person. The leader. And the secret of leadership – if there is one – is a great ability to improve people. The improving method is not the key to leadership. The style is. How you engage people is.

An orchestra has several people and instruments. A good leader has to play the part of the conductor. The conductor watches the characteristics of each member and tries to integrate them on the team. Some in a smoother way, others more abruptly. The leader must empower people, in a constant search of the best for the team.

José Mourinho and Pep Guardiola are followed and admired by a large population. And from those, not everyone does it for football related matters or because they are managers of their teams. They are also followed for matters related to leadership. Watching their videos, analysing their speeches, reading his works, all of this bring us knowledge. Allows us to compare styles and analyse the results. And we are not just talking about sports results, but also about the commitment, satisfaction and return their players provide.

Directly managing over thirty people, if we count a squad and the close members of the technical team, is not easy at all. And we are talking about leadership on site. At a competition level that does not allow errors, or at least many errors, since they would bring several serious consequences and almost always negative ones. To analyse these two managers using different theories is highly endearing.

Their leadership is different, of course! If we think that leadership includes the individual characteristics of the leader, his behaviours, beliefs, and feelings, as well as situational and contextual issues, we understand that we can find some similar patterns in some managers, however equal patterns are quite impossible to find. In this case it is easy to see that they are different, and in certain cases almost or totally the opposite.

Two researchers, Chelladurai e Saleh[10], presented in 1980 a scale of leadership in sports with five types of management leadership behaviour. It has evolved, but there is a need to have something that keeps up with the behavioural and cognitive changes of being a manager. Until that happens, what those two authors profiled were the following five groups of behaviours with five categories:

---

[10] *Chelladurai, P. & Saleh, S. D. (1980) in Lança, R. & Lopes, M. (2015)*

- Social support (satisfies the personal needs of the group members);
- Training and education (improvement of the athlete's performance);
- Positive reaction (rewards good performance);
- Democratic behaviour (including members of the group in the decision making process);
- Autocratic behaviour (to act independently in the decision making process).

These behaviours lead to three dimensions: one addressing the task (coaching and instructive behaviour), another two styles of decision making(autocratic and democratic behaviour) and a third dimension for the two motivational factors (positive feed-back and social support).

By the end of the 70s/beginning of the 80s, several theories emerged related to the act of leading a group aiming to get the most of it. The theory of charismatic leadership (House, 1977);the theory of transformational and transactional leadership (Bass, 1985; Bass & Avolio, 1994); the theories of visionary leadership developed by several authors between 1985 and 1990.

When analysing the two coaches, we believe that they fit in a scenery of behaviours and beliefs that can be included in the transformational leadership, since it transforms the goals of the athletes or convinces them to leave their individual goals, not exactly to second plan, but at least aligned and complementary to those of the team. Thus the leader manages to commit the athletes in a way that they understand that if their goals are aligned with those of the team, they will be easily attainable if the team goals are achieved.

This theory of transformational leadership is quite relevant to study the sports leadership, especially due to the empathic ability the leader is able to create in the relationship and to change the athletes' behaviours and beliefs. This type of shared leadership has a greater influence if they lead by example. This theory claims that leadership behaviour goes from passive and not very effective, to active and effective.

They also present good motivational abilities leading to a more optimistic vision towards the performances that are achieved. Optimistic not as a goal being easy to reach, but optimistic towards the performances that the members involved are able to obtain.

Although this is one of the less explored fields, we consider that Mourinho and Guardiola get a great part of their success with their teams from their ability to include their players in the problem solving process, and to develop in their athletes and teams the intelligence to perceive the constrains and practical intelligence. Finally, when taking part of shared leadership, each athlete increases the level of consideration for their piers when understanding their needs, hence increasing the cooperation levels, the group vision of the goals, strengths and weaknesses of the team.

When reading these theories, although later analysed in a more academic way with past cases of sports and society, we recall the words of the former president of the United States, John Quincy Adams (1767-1848:

> *"If your actions inspire others to dream more, learn more, do more and be more, then you are a leader."*

Other related theme that is often mentioned is the expression "to be charismatic". When we say this word, it comes to mind the image of Mourinho throughout his path, from Oporto to Madrid. Running around the court after winning the UEFA cup to the Portuguese club; enjoying himself with his family at the German stadium after his first victory in the Champions League; the way he celebrated in Santiago Barnabéu in his second Champions League when he was still at Inter. And, of course, running around the stadium, which is going to be his again, celebrating the goal of the Portuguese midfielder Costinha which gave him a straight pass to the semi-finals of the Champions League 2003/04 he ended up winning.

Jorge Costa recalls what he thinks about Mourinho, which can be aligned with charismatic leadership[11]:

> *"How does he cause this? I don't know... you feel it. It is almost like when you fall in love with someone and love is difficult to explain, isn't it? The bottom line is that these are such pure, such natural relationships that they are difficult to explain."*

The charismatic theory aims to analyse the characteristics of the leader that lead to actions through which he obtains results and high performances. And one of the first characteristics was charisma.

When you think of charisma, people with a very reliable way of being come to mind. People transmitting confidence. People that when we look at them we know beforehand that their decisions are correct, effective and reasoned, even if it is just because of their experience and analysis abilities. However, could they be charismatic and at the same time passionate in the way they relate to others? Yes. Although literature analyses charisma in leadership and leaders being emotionally active as being in the same axis and, therefore, in opposite directions, truth is that charisma sits well with passion!

These two managers are passionate about what they do. And, even so, they could be introverted within the group they work with. But they are not and assume the real importance of being authentic, of emotionally being able to make their players express sentences of pure love, of making them cry with joy due to the examples they set. A major factor in nowadays leadership. Even in a world that most of the time does not have space for error!

---

[11] *Lourenço, L. (2010)*

These examples help and reinforce two points:

Lets imagine Mourinho running along the side-lines to celebrate with his athletes. Kissing his players. Running to his children. Cursing out loud in his mother language. Guardiola saying to Philipp Lahm: "I love you, thank you for your performance" or talking with the French Ribery with him replying: "I love you, you are in my heart!". When the Danish midfielder, Pierre-Emile Hojbjerg, confided to Guardiola that his father suffered from cancer, both cried. The coach tried to help his athlete every way he could, but the player's father died a few months later. Pierre-Emile Hojbjerg assumed that "Pep is like a second father to me".

- In leadership there aren't exactly recipes and therefore beliefs and suppositions never experienced in our reality are in the first place fears or malpractices of the leader.
- There are actions that, in general, get better results, and other actions that, in general, get bad results. But even so, it is necessary and essential that these reasons are analysed and that the whole process is deconstructed so that we can understand what we achieved and what we didn't.

To analyse leadership and leaders' behaviour is a complex task. We want to be sure that our statements and analysis are as accurate as possible. But they always have to be based on different fields. We can observe someone performing something and from that take information about what that person, a leader or not, does, executes, their cognitions. Talking with those leaders we are able to understand what they think about a wide variety of issues brought into the conversation. We can infer what they feel under certain circumstances.

And then you have the side of the led. To question what they think about what the coaches, the leaders, think and verbalize. What they feel it has been accomplished and what are the goals.

Situations they consider leadership to be less fluid or consistent. To analyse leadership and not the results but the behavioural processes, will always have the complexity and the need of filling in the gaps between what the leader thinks he does, thinks, and feels, and the vision of the other side, the athletes and the teams. Knowing beforehand that the vision, subjectivity, and filter of each of the human beings involved is something quite intricate.

Try to simplify is understanding that each leader can be analysed under the following parameters:

What he does	What he thinks	What he feels
COGNITIONS	**BELIEFS**	**FEELINGS**

The words of Deco about his work with the Portuguese coach are quite enlightening:

> *"We were a very strong group, but also very United, and we weren't just good players, we also had high human quality. Then we wanted to win, we had a huge ambition for victory. That ambition was natural and at a personal level, but besides that, Mourinho managed to create a group ambition and thus we enjoyed training, playing, be together, we did it with pleasure."* [12]

Jack Welch, an excellent CEO, fits the knowhow of leaders within eight tasks, adapted to sports:

1. Leaders are constantly improving the level of their team, making each match an opportunity to evaluate, guide (coach) and build up self-trust.

2. Leaders assure that their team does not only know and is aware of the vision, but they live it and breathe it.

3. Leaders get into everyone and convey positive energy and optimism.

---

[12] *Lourenço, L. (2010)*

4. Leaders build trust with honesty, transparency and consideration.

5. Leaders have the courage to assume unpopular positions, and follow their intuition.

6. Leaders search and encourage with a curiosity that touches scepticism, assuring that their questions are answered with actions.

7. Leaders encourage learning and taking risks, setting the example.

8. Leaders celebrate.

Using an advice from Pep and Mourinho, we must resort to the best in order to learn. And there are more similarities than differences between the several sporting categories. The only thing that changes is the restrains. And the contexts. We resort to one of the best managers ever and expert in mind games and leadership, Phil Jackson. He is one of the managers with more NBA rings and coached a couple of the best athletes ever in group games, like Michael Jordan, Koby Bryant, and Scottie Pippen. What he shares with other managers and the public are eleven lessons with simple examples of the high level leadership of American basketball (NBA):

1. As time went by, I discovered that the more I spoke from the heart, the more players could hear me and benefit from what I gleaned.

2. I need to dial back my ego and distribute power as widely as possible without surrendering final authority.

3. My approach was always to relate to each player as a whole person, not just a cog in the basketball machine. That meant pushing him to discover what distinct qualities he could bring to the game beyond taking shots and making passes. How much courage did he have? Or resilience? What about character under fire? Many

players I've coached didn't look special on paper, but in the process of creating a role for themselves they grew into formidable champions.

4. The road to freedom is a beautiful system. All must be fully engaged every second — or the whole system will fail.

5. Offer the players other realities and occupy their minds with other subjects outside the sport.

6. Phil he created mindfulness for his teams so they could better connect with one another, preparing them for the teamwork needed on the court. If you place too many restrictions on players, they'll spend an inordinate amount of time trying to buck the system. Like all of us, they need a certain degree of structure in their lives, but they also require enough latitude to express themselves creatively.

7. Compassion – although it isn't a very used word – is one of the keys to success.

8. Keep your eye on the spirit, not on the scoreboard. I preferred to focus my attention on whether the players were moving together in a spirited way.

9. Prepares them for the difference Not because I want to make their lives miserable but because I want to prepare them for the inevitable chaos that occurs the minute they step onto a court.

10. We have to accept that there are occasions when the best solution is to do absolutely nothing.

11. Sometimes the best way to fight for success is to forget what we already achieved, even so we can enjoy the game again.

Another key point in the marriage between structure and leadership is the ability of fitting together the mission and vision with passion. And possibly Pep and Barcelona were the perfect marriage. But as former Blaugrana president Rossel stated, "There was a life before Guardiola arrived to Barcelona and life will continue when he leaves."

It might be pure speculation, but we think that Barcelona found another almost perfect partner to replace Guardiola in an easier way than the other way around. Pep found in Catalonia the perfect conditions to develop his ideas, even if he did an excellent work in Munich. But in Bavarian lands, the coach stumbled on some internal obstacles, while Catalonia was almost wonderland for Guardiola.

And what has this to do with leadership? A lot! To be a leader is not a timeless position. It is something that you conquer, a daily challenge. And to overcome that challenge, the institution has to search for someone who has the skills to meet its values, the institutional and work philosophy in order to achieve its goals. As for the manager, it is not enough to have a lot of skills. Not even the best skills. He has to have those that meet the needs and visions of the institution. And here we understand why there are leaders who fit like a glove in the project of the institution, the club, and the team. Guardiola and Barcelona were like that. Let's wait and find out how it will be in the City!

Time always comes up when talking about projects. The time coaches have to implement their ideas. In a League where only one can win – as usual – but where the charges for the losers will be higher than the investment. The daily fight of procedures and results. As John Wooden claimed while manager, leaders know that they don't have all the time of the world to leave their personal brand in the game and leadership. He left us the following quote, which summarises the new wave of coaches:

> "When we improve on a daily basis, good things start to happen. We should not aim to do everything great and fast, but search for a little improvement every day. It is the only way for things to happen. And when it happens, it lasts."

Soriano[13], former Vice-President of Barcelona, based on his experience in management and sports, gave us four types of leader, according to the technical contents and ability:

+	Authoritarian Experienced	Coach
Content	Political Dictator	Facilitator
–	**– Capacity**	**+**

Soriano also claims that charisma is a vital quality for someone who wants to lead a group, although being useful to gain the leadership of the group or in hard times, when the trust of the group is needed and tough decisions are to be made.

It is interesting how he differentiates leadership and charisma, when he states that leadership is the only condition to be a leader, while charisma refers to the quality or moral ability of a person to guide others with no type of coercion. He adds that the key point of leadership and charisma is the entitlement of those showing off or taking advantage of that factor. To last it has to obtain results every day.

Northouse defines leadership as a procedure and experience interaction between leaders and led to reach a common goal. It may include formal leaders (coaches, team, captains) and informal leaders, depending of the role within the team. Based on this definition, we highlight four core components of leadership:

---

[13] *Soriano, F. (2009)*

1. Leadership is an interaction process between the leader and the followers, thus being the leader affected by the followers and vice-versa;
2. The leader influences and might affect his followers;
3. Leadership occurs in groups;
4. Leadership focus on reaching goals and manage to guide a group to reach them.[14]

In a more traditional point of view, leadership used to be seen as what was given to the team, skills and behaviours and other components like charisma that might have a direct impact on the team processes and performance. Today, leadership is mainly analysed by the results and outcomes of the team. The ability to lead teams is interpreted as an emergent stage or the building of something that develops the team in medium and long term, like a dynamic second nature and varying with the processes, inclusions and results.

Individuals
• Behavioural and task skills
• Experience
• Individual and group focus and alignment

Leader behaviours	**Leadership effectiveness**
• Ability to clarify the vision and goal	• Ability to motivate and improve the performance of the athlete
• Guide to achieve the goal	
• Facilitate the task, relationships and decision taking	• Way how to make oneself accepted (recognition or imposition)
• Abide to group rules	
• Belief, values, and cognitions	• Individual, individual + group, and group performance

Environment and Context

---

[14] *Northouse, P. G. (2014) in Lança, R. & Lopes, M. (2015)*

The team leaders have great influence in what the team generates or isn't able to produce. The team leaders (formal or emerging) create, encourage and develop a feeling of sharing through an effective team work and must create an environment which encourages adaptability.

In an interview by Sitkin and Hackman[15] to one of the best Basketball coaches ever, Mike Krzyzewski, with several individual and group titles, both with his University and the USA national team, Coach K, as he is known, stated that team leadership:

> *"is plural, not singular; hence there can be more than one leader (...) although not everyone on the team is or wants to be a leader".*

Taking into account some statements, it is easy to understand that the positive and fruitful alignment Pep managed to get in Barcelona is hard to obtain anywhere else. But even because of that, it must be quite challenging for people who ask a lot from themselves. Like Pep does. The Bulgarian star and former Blaugrana player, Hristo Stoichkov, stated at some point that Guardiola was the last of the Mohicans of the Cruyff era: "We are never going to have another manager able to win six titles in a single season, it is almost impossible".

When Pep left Catalonia, Messi wrote on his Facebook page: "I want to thank Pep from the bottom of my heart for everything he gave me, both personally and professionally." Finally, one of his hardest opponents to beat, the Portuguese Mourinho and now rival from the other side of town, stated when he was at Real Madrid, that "Guardiola is the best manager for the Barcelona".

Pep also loves analogies between football and chess. He tries to understand his opponents as if he were in a chess game, he finds the idea fascinating. Each time he reads something about chess he tries to draw a parallel between the two sports.

---

15 *Sitkin, S. & Hackman, J. (2011)*

On the other hand, both Mourinho and Guardiola work a lot. They want to be the best, but more than the talent of knowing what to do, they want to know how to behave and abide to group rules, so that they fit a set of patterns to which everyone should be aligned within the sacred locker rooms of each team. Guardiola, surround by excellence, contests the need of putting aside excellence as something that brings previously attained results:

> "Excellence. What exactly is excellence? Excellence is like a bubble. You can look for it as much as you like but it only appears from time to time. You have to be ready, you have to be at the right place and prepared for the opportunities."

His friend Sala i Martin would define Guardiola as obsessive. The word "might be considered as passion and an extreme detail in preparation". Guardiola likes a quote of Cavafy from the famous poem 'Íthaca' "It makes the journey long", to which Guardiola added "Lets also hope that it will be a good journey too".

At the time of a qualifier between Benfica and Bayern Munich, with a 2-2 tie allowing the Bavarian team trained by Guardiola to get to the semi-finals of the Champions League, a Spanish journalist asked Pep Guardiola at the Luz Stadium auditorium: "Xabi Alonso said that both you and Mourinho have similar personalities, what do you have to say about that?". Guardiola took a deep breath and gave a short answer. "Xabi Alonso knows both me and José Mourinho. I don't have much to say about that."

We don't know the analysis degree of this statement of the Spanish midfielder. We don't know if he wanted to be politically correct or if he gave his honest opinion. But one of the more exciting issues of the leadership of a coach is exactly to understand if what it reaches the players is what the coach intends to transmit.

And, judging by the several researches on the area, what a coach builds on him always gets a subjectivity degree that can be more or less depending of countless issues. From the mental ability and organisation of the coach, the way he processes information, what type of information he collects, and the assertiveness degree towards himself, and the one his athletes, assistants, and managers have towards him.

Arrigo Sacchi states about the Portuguese:

> "I love Mourinho. He is a great coach, a unique coach. He has an inner force, a capacity, a charisma, personality, clear ideas, high level of knowledge. He's big. His theory tells it."

Xabier Azkargorta, a renowned manager, claims that Mourinho is an "endurance runner" and Guardiola a "sprinter", because the Portuguese "has more grey hair and more sacrifice in his career. He conquered the management world in all its aspects, he wasn't famous as player, he was translator, assistant and informer, and his path was longer and more diversified, like an endurance runner." The Catalan "on the other hand, appeared like a devastator sprinter in the coaching world, approved by his charisma and is fame as an icon professional player of Barça."

We leave here an advice, being sure that coaches and leaders like Mourinho and Guardiola do it constantly, as a result of how much they demand of themselves and being aware of the importance of being several steps ahead: to give an answer to three simple questions:

What I want to do	What I want to think	What I want to feel
COGNITIONS	**BELIEFS**	**FEELINGS**

Not as self-manipulation, but as a way – in their minds – to be prepared with the appropriated skills they consider to be the best according to the environments and challenges.

Shared Leadership

When analysing both coaches, Pep Guardiola is very much connected to what researchers call shared leadership. In sports, this may influence and promote the commitment of the players through encouragement, example or sharing the decision making process. Mike Krzyzewski, for instance, considers that it is easier for the managers who trust themselves to share that leadership in order to encourage players, without this meaning that not sharing represents lack of self-trust.

Although we consider Mourinho being more controlling than Guardiola (see scheme), the Portuguese as a quite interesting opinion about what this guided discovery may be – an expression that came up quite strongly and is often used in rugby –, containing a lot of leadership empowerment within the learning process and skills acquisition:

> "My guided discovery has more to do with feeling than with seeing, that is, what the players feel in a certain situation or movement. I ask them what they feel at an experimentation level... let's try to feel that I am supported at a positional level... at a mental level that I am not afraid to fail because it is covered... And this is our starting point, we do the training and I get the feedback which allows me to make changes accordingly. And that flexibility, the ability to make changes within the training based on what they tell me. If I understand from what they say, the exercise is not suitable to the situation I immediately change it. Sometimes, after three minutes, I have already introduced a new rule to the exercise, so that I can adapt it to what the players are feeling. Deep down it is also operationalization directly connected to a guided discovery."[16]

---

[16] *Lourenço, L. (2010)*

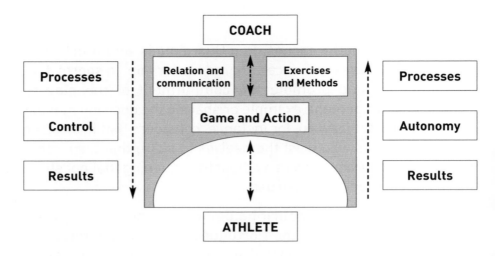

The better the shared leadership (in conscience when shared by the leaders), more efficient are the teams, but never forgetting that the relationship between coach and athlete is a hierarchical relationship, and when an individual is recognised as a leader, there is also an open mind towards the use of behavioural control, something you can perceive in some of José Mourinho's talks.

In shared leadership, the influence is distributed to the team members, instead of being concentrated in just one. In these teams the members can be either leaders or led at different moments and areas, according to the context and goals.

The question of this table is: Where does Mourinho fit in? And Guardiola, considering the knowledge we have on these two coaches? And you while coach and leader of a group?

Watching this scale it is possible to fit both coaches. Even because high performance athletes explicitly prefer coaches who are oriented towards instruction behaviour. The question is to understand how they execute it and what type of behaviours come with the instruction. We can see a more relaxed Pep, showing more smiles, but also more anxious. Mourinho is more like and actor and more controlling than he shows. A more passionate Pep, a more pragmatic Mourinho. Guardiola and Mourinho are innovators but in different areas of the field.

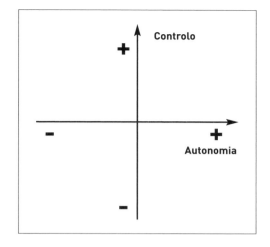

We could point out more differences, but we believe that these new episodes of the English League will confirm some of these behaviours, as well as the possibility to find out who will leave his comfort zone first.

Teams with high levels of shared leadership change and rotate throughout time at different points of their life cycles and their development. Patterns of mutual influence are created and strengthen the relationships between the members of the team, which is positive. For shared leadership to emerge, the team members have to be opened to lead and manage to influence the direction, motivation and support of the group.

Moreover the team, as a whole, has to search for leadership for different members, thus they have to accept and believe in themselves and in others. The internal environment is an essential factor. There must be support for that type of leadership to emerge and exist and that the level of support from the trainer comes from the support of an external leader, like some of the athletes in Mourinho's and Guardiola's teams that lead on the field.

It is not difficult to suggest that in Porto teams both Jorge Costa and Costinha were basic pillars inside the pitch. Terry, Lampard or Drogba in Chelsea. Cambiasso in Inter. As for Guardiola's teams, Lahm was always the player who stood out in Munich, due to the total trust and freedom to lead Pep gave the German player, and in Barcelona, players like Xavi or Iniesta always took the role of being his arms and mind on the field.

Shared leadership is related to other concepts, like team autonomy, self-management, proactive teams, emerging cooperation and leadership, however it is important to point out that it is different from all of these, being closer to autonomous or self-management teams.

Shared leadership is more noticeable in Guardiola's teams than in Mourinho's, it is a characteristic of an emerging team resulting from the distribution of leadership among the several members of the team. It represents an incorporated (given) condition of mutual influence among the team members which can clearly improve performance, both individual and of the team.

At this level, coaches are immensely and intensely demanding. Always searching for something different and better. Guardiola, besides having one of the best water polo players in his technical team, he enjoyed meeting with the basketball coach of Bayern Munich to discuss matters that could be transposed from one sport to the other, like the defence or the way the athletes occupied all spaces on the field. For the Catalan coach there is a "(...) concern about understanding and give to the athletes the tactical concepts of the game and the sport. This takes a big part of my day."

The narrative of a leader

"Football is such a complicated game that you become coach because you want to control it. You believe that you master it with what you do and what you say, but it is impossible to dominate, except if you are Messi."

Pep Guardiola

"I want to train for another 15 years. I am going to win more titles. Two fingers are missing for having two full hands, but I still have 10 toes."

José Mourinho

Those who teach and lead others tend to carry out activities to convince themselves that there is a correct way of thinking, feeling and acting. Kind of making sense of the narrative we create and which allow us a suitable place where we examine identity and allowing us to live with the existing ambiguities and contradictions, many of them exterior but also inside our own mind.

It also allows the narrative author to explain his point of view about something and realise that when he tells his history, someone else's history or another important event, he has the advantage of using his own filters to positively influence the time, cultural, historic or spatial information he wants to convey and that this same information is absorbed as the narrator wishes.

When we are talking about a manager's leadership, we can divide it into two tasks: understanding by the voice of the manager what are the beliefs, actions and feelings of the leader; and after understanding which are the interpretations, opinions and practical cases of his players or managers, knowing beforehand that either of the interventions will always carry the subjectivity of the visions and interpretations of a human being.

We know from the opinions of José Mourinho and Pep Guardiola, and of those working with them, that they are both two very demanding managers. And professional. But you don't get where they got and win what they won without these skills. And much more!

One of the skills that have been studied about successful coaches and leaders is their narration ability. And what might this translate into in the narrative of José Mourinho and Pep Guardiola?

Let us take a look at these two paragraphs taken from an interview by José Mourinho to Reader´s Digest magazine, where he states that he prefers to be recognised for his personal interactions and leadership, by acknowledging the individuality of each:

> *"That's more like it. Performing authority will fade in time and with the empathy I build up. When I arrive to a club I feel the need to show who I am and what I can do; I need to make a statement and establish some rules. My leadership, everyone feels it but no one sees it. Having chosen an education made me a better coach. Coaches nowadays have to search for knowledge."*

> *"A football coach who only knows about football is a lousy football coach" and because of that he asks around for everything. There are scientific areas that may help us in our work, namely psychology, pedagogy, physiology. I can talk to my medical department about lesions, muscles, biomechanics, coaching theory. Those are subjects I master. To master the psychological skills is essential. It can make a difference."*

When we read those paragraphs we can focus in what the Portuguese coach says he likes and his vision of leadership. But not only that. While reading we can also question how Mourinho arrived to these conclusions? To this set of clear ideas and conclusions about himself? Did it take long to get there? Would these sentences get the attention of an athlete or a manager? To this we can call building our own image, not to tap on our back and feel good with ourselves, but to build something logical and that embraces several factors which are becoming increasingly important in team leadership!

The atmosphere a manager is able to create through is personal interaction influences the athlete's behaviour and that relationship is built upon communication, either verbal, written, postural or symbolic. The coach must incorporate in his communication and action a consistency and an essential effectiveness, hence the importance of being prepared; of creating and identity or a brand; of knowing how to transfer, create and practice his rhetoric, in a way that will help to reach his goals. Even though we might not like the path taken to achieve the goals, one thing is certain, managers live mostly on results, and "the results vouch for Mourinho", like Xavi Hernández stated.

Just think that most people, and probably many of us, just remember some coaches (just sticking to sports) due to the more newsworthy results they reached throughout their careers. Just those who are really interested on the subject think they know how those coaches and leaders reached success.

Back to the narrative, some authors analyse the issue of dilemma, faces or paranoia of a coach through the stories they build and live. The coach is increasingly exposed, even because football, in this case, is keeping the media attention, and that is clearly a risk. The relationship of each coach with his identity brings some tension and anxiety, and at the same time opens doors to enthusiasm and introspection. We must keep in mind that the interactions between a manager and his players are coated by an emotional intensity, essential to create a connection with the audience, and not only with the athletes.

It is not new, but it is quite interesting to see that when coaches create their social image worry about their interviews, about the moments they speak about themselves, because they know it is important to create an impact on those listening to them. Some call it mind games, others call it concern with the communicational impact, but all of it fits in the coach's philosophy – a statement on the manager's characteristics and on the way he thinks and acts.

This philosophy has a direct impact on his behaviour and many coaches fail this commitment to adapt their behavioural philosophy in order to solve their daily problems. Worse of all is that the coaches do not invest in the process of developing and clarifying a philosophy and its verbalization for the context they are in.

Mourinho e Guardiola are an exception due to the amazing ability they have shown throughout their careers, being consistent in what they say and with what their players say they do. These two coaches work a lot on this area, although it seems to us that the Portuguese invests more. We don't mean to say this is better, but that he "rehearses" and worries more about the impact of his words, while the Catalan looks more spontaneous.

A good personal definition of the action philosophy is much valuable and it may get good actions and reactions. Thus, the philosophy based on principles must be reliable and useful for the coach, but also flexible enough to be aware of the existing contextual factors. The expression "life history" is a search method with a rich potential which allows for introspection in order to help the coach's performance. One of the main advantages of this introspection is the possibility of putting the individual subjectivity of reality and to use it on the field.

The phenomenon of the personal brand is very close to movements to sell an idea, something that embodies the person and may be considered a strategy to obtain more success in his work. Although the idea may be limited on sales terms, the truth is that success is not determined by the set of internal skills, motivations or interests, but in fact by the way they are organised and worked out, that is, embodied with an identity. Associated to the personal brand, which always implies a working and life style model, in this case of a manager, we can find rhetoric that encourages and re-inforces the process of turning its contents in something easier to commit to by the issuer and the receiver.

We have to admit that narrative is all over the place when we talk about speeches. And that the neutral speech "thing" does not exist from the moment that there is a sender and a wish to influ-ence an audience. For instance, speaking with students about practice implies using different pedagogies and transmitting knowledge in a different way, always adapting. These words may cause some dislike but, either you want it or not, the word per-suasion is implicit in the task of transmitting knowledge and a message.

"Until the beginning of the training I have two hours of absolute tran-quillity so that, in the silence of my office, I can prepare in detail the working session specified according to the analysis"[17]. These are José Mourinho words. When we say this is a narrative, it is because we consider these words will help us understand the requirement and dedication of a professional who reached the top. Dedication allied to passion for what you do and for your goals. The Portuguese coach likes to arrive early to the training centre, because it allows him to work calmly, in the solitude of being a manager, and let his ideas flow, leaving us some clues about the sometimes lonely way that comes together with a manager's career. Personal responsi-bility and self-management are necessary.

Let us see another statement of Mourinho: "Before training I still have time for a briefing with my watchers for a perfect identifica-tion of the next opponent; with the person in charge of the pitch considering the weather conditions; assistants in charge of the training support material; with the doctor to evaluate the clinical condition and definition of the plan for the injured (...)". This list

---

[17] *Luz, N. & Pereira, L. M. (2011)*

of tasks he performs or likes to pay attention to could even be longer.

Next we will take the words of one of the athletes who knows him well. Maniche, European champion with Mourinho, says: "He likes to be involved in everything. He's a gardener, driver, security... he likes to keep everything under control and pays attention to details. He thinks about the team 24 hours a day". And this is it. The rhetoric of a leader can be confirmed as previously stated: the comparison between what, in this case, Mourinho says about himself, about his cognitions and feelings, and what is transmitted to us by his athletes.

Some managers have no problem admitting that they want their team to be their mirror in what concerns organisation. Others not that much. Not everyone has the rhetorical ability to express themselves and make the speech about themselves similar to that of the player defining his coach. It is not about judging if it is a good or bad manager, but more like if he is able to be transparent and authentic enough to transmit what he wanted to transmit. Mourinho and Guardiola do it and this plays clearly in favour of these managers.

"Things have to get worse before they get better" – This was one of the beliefs of Guardiola during his first months in Bayern Munich. When a new manager arrives, it doesn't matter how good he is. Pep knew he was going to replace another great manager who had done a lot for the German club. Pep thought it was normal that the team lost confidence, security and dynamics. "You need time and persistence to recover it all, to get better and bigger. The losses are the price you pay for progress" those were his words. These could be defined as beliefs of the Catalan manager. And the way he convinced himself of these same ideas. And those listening to him. Being those journalists, German managers or his athletes.

When he was criticized for these statements, Guardiola answered and this was his belief:

"You may criticize me how and where you want. But you are never going to be as critical as I am of myself." About the way he played he answered: *"My way of playing is my way of playing. Of course there are several ways to reach success. It is not relevant if my way is the best way. But it is mine."*

Mourinho accepts to do an interesting exercise speaking in a thorough way about his leadership[18]:

"What does being a leader mean to me?For me to lead is not to give orders, for me to lead is to guide. I am going to make a parallel with parenthood so I can explain it better. You can be a father who gives orders or you can be a father who guides. Now, what happens today is that any father tries that his children learn by themselves, finding their way without any need to give them orders. When you give orders you castrate. I go with my son treasure hunting. In the first place, I am not going to tell him where the treasure is, because the game would lose all its effectiveness, not only of leisure but also as educational. He has to make an effort to find the treasure; he has to do what he can, little by little, to collect the necessary leads to find it. When he does, through the leads I gave him, he is happy because it was him who found it, I didn't tell him where it was. If I had told him at the beginning, I would have castrated a series of skills which, sooner or later, would make him discover a treasure and give another step towards his formation as a human being."

This testimony is fantastic for several reasons. Not just because it is the vision of Mourinho on how to be a leader. His beliefs and speaking about some of his actions. And even the feeling to watch someone being able to grow and develop some skills, but it is – as stated – the vision, and only that, of Mourinho about himself!

---

[18] *Lourenço, L. (2010)*

The Communication

"If you love what you do, you won't lose your hair.
See Guardiola who is bald, that means he doesn't
like football."

José Mourinho

"Talent depends on inspiration, the effort depends of each one."

Pep Guardiola

José Mourinho and Pep Guardiola are two colossi also in what concerns communication. Their words are always heard and achieve a great impact inside and outside of the scope of their teams. One more executive, the other more empathic, their words and messages have, almost always, more than one direction. Not only their players or the journalists, but they also include their direct and indirect opponents, with José Mourinho being more strategic and making more use of this technique.

Indeed, the Portuguese stated that "when I am going to a press conference before the match, in my head the match has already started." An Italian journalist said about José Mourinho, when he was managing Inter Milan, that "All this is a game, a theatre where he puts his mask on and takes it off when it is convenient for him." Alex Ferguson defines Mourinho as an excellent communicator: "I always considered him as being very much available and communicative. I think he understood he was dealing with someone that had already lived all the extremes of football and appreciated our conversations."

On his first public day of work in the Manchester United, the Portuguese wind up / communicated like he likes to do:

> "To hide myself behind words and philosophies, I have never been good at it. I have always been aggressive in my approach with all the risks that this entails. Let's work and try and be back to the Champions League, try and be back to the top four. I prefer to be more aggressive and say we want to win. I can anticipate any one of you will come later with a question about style of play [...] I can anticipate [...] you cannot win competitions without playing well."

If we think about theatre, Pep also mentioned that in one of his conferences. And it depicts well those theatrical moments. Not in the sense they are fake, but in the sense of playing a part that everyone is anxious to analyse, consume or merely enjoy:

> "When I am facing the press or the players there is an imposing element, almost theatrical, in order to be able to reach them. But in the end, I always transmit what I feel. There is an element of shame, of fear, of acting the fool that makes me contain myself a little, then there is what I have learnt from football and the thing is that it scares me to make a statement when I know that the game is uncontrollable, that tomorrow my words can come back and haunt me. That false humility that people say I have, always giving the players the credit, isn't because I don't want to acknowledge my own merits, it's because I panic about having those words turned on me. Because by doing exactly the same as what I am doing now, I could lose tomorrow."

If we think what really is included in the act of communicating between two or more people, and we add to that a hierarchical position, this will be perhaps the base of leading procedures and teams, together with personal interaction. And it becomes even more important since there can't be any fails or lacks of communication, when the communication isn't made in the first language of those wanting to assume the control of the dialogue.

Presently teams speak several languages. Mourinho speaks well his first language, Portuguese, and expresses himself quite well in English and Italian due to the years he coached in those countries, as well as in Spanish, a language that the Portuguese easily get. But in a training of Real Madrid, Chelsea or the Red Devils, there may be also the Dutch, French or German, among others.

The Manchester City of the 2015/16 season was a multicultural and language festival for all tastes. Pep Guardiola speaks Spanish and Catalan, what became handy in Barcelona. And it can be useful to have a conversation in more stressful environments or to level the conversation with the sports manager now in the Citizens. But in Munich Pep had to talk several times in German, English, Spanish, French or Italian. Of course that both Pep and José or any other coach resort to gestures when verbal communication is not enough. The face expressions, the hand gestures and all the posture of the body. The main issue is not letting the passion fade by the fact they are speaking another language with which they don't feel comfortable.

José Mourinho is the author of several famous sentences. The first with great impact came up at his presentation in Chelsea back in 2004, when he stated: "Please don't call me arrogant, but I'm a European Champion and I think I am someone special". From then on he started being called the Special One, until he returned the second time to London and started being called the Happy One.

Guardiola is a bit different. More spontaneous, although he changed a bit during his stay on Bavarian lands. At the bench during the games, Guardiola has more energy. He signs a lot and stands most of the time. He hugs and pushes. One of the most remarkable episodes, which was observed in a very explicit way, happened right after he was going to the City and the German championship was almost guaranteed, in a victory and after the match ended, he entered the pitch to speak to the German player Kimmich about the corrections needed and made the athlete mimic his body movements, following his lead.

The Catalan has an interesting statement and self-analysis concerning the way to communicate:

> *"I was a player and I know what I am talking about. In all conversations, I put my heart in communications. When I am not able to feel what I am about to say I won't say it. It is the best way. There are days when you think that you have something to say, but if you aren't feeling it, you better stay quiet."*

José Mourinho is a manager who was for along time the best football manager using this tool as a way to send messages everywhere he wanted. He did it in an almost perfect way, managing being an actor more often, letting feelings and emotions show, generating actions crucial for the result (not only sportive) he wanted to get.

An example of the mastery of Mourinho in communicating and jump stages of what could be communicational issues, was the strategy he started to use when he was still in FC Porto when he gave small pieces of paper to the athlete that entered the pitch as replacement. We recall the first episodes in Chelsea when he gave the Portuguese player Tiago a piece of paper to give to one of his mates on the pitch. This caught the attention of the English media.

What could that be? A simple way to communicate with someone distant and above all, the need to reduce the noise that would be created by telling something to the Portuguese player for him to transmit to his mate of other nationality and speaking another language. Naturally the midfielder would always introduce another word or transmit the message in a more emotional or rational way. With this small gesture, Mourinho took out of the way what could have been a change to his message.

Costinha, one of his players in Porto said: "What I know is that he communicates with you in such a deep and convincing way that you feel like reacting, even after being harshly yelled at like I was". Another athlete of Mourinho and player of the Portuguese club FC Porto, Jorge Costa, stated: "He is straightforward and effective in the way he communicates; you can feel the reliability of his speech, the secure way of his speech."

When we read the statements of the Portuguese players, we almost feel like comparing them, in a different scope, to the words of António Damásio and the ability excellent managers have to address each athlete in a very empathic way:

> "The reader is looking at this page, reading this text and reasoning the meaning of my words as he progresses. However, what is going on inside his mind is no way limited to the text or its meaning. In parallel to the representation of the printed words and the recall of concepts needed to understand what I wrote, his mind reveals also another thing, something that is enough to show, at each moment that it is the who is reading and understanding the text reader and not someone else. The images corresponding to his external perceptions and the perceptions of what he recalls occupy almost the full extension of his mind, but not all of it. Besides these images, there is also another presence that makes you, while spectator of imagined things, owner of the imagined things and potential actor on the imagined things. (...) If this presence wouldn't exist, how could you know the thoughts belonged to you?"

Communication has been one of the pillars of the best coaches in different sports. Both Mourinho and Guardiola admired basketball and NBA coaches as a way to learn best practices. Two of the best coaches were Phil Jackson and Michael Krzyzewsky. The first, during his career as coach of the Chicago Bulls and the LA Lakers, where he got several rings (titles) of the American Professional Basketball League, NBA, demanded from his players the following: "Is like I say to my children, always ask. Don't assume, ask". The second coach of the American national selection claimed that "Team work begins and ends in communication".

Sala i Martin consider that Guardiola has an easy and accessible speech:

> "He doesn't use complicated words. He is a normal guy and uses simple words. He is a simple person, coming from a humble family and hasn't forgot his origins."

...ioanalyst once stated about José Mourinho's communication and its reach:

> *"You have to understand that almost every conversation Mourinho
> has are part of his work, and that the ultimate end of those commu-
> nications is not communication per se, but to increase the odds for
> his team's victories. At a press conference, he is not talking to the
> people in room, other coaches, FA and so forth. The advice I would
> give is the sports equivalent to what all the political interviewers
> should ask themselves: "why is this lying bastard lying to me?" "*

While training during the pre-season in Scotland with his
Barcelona, Guardiola prepared for another talk. The team was
aligned in the room like in a classroom. Not much space between
each of the elements in there. Players, medical team, assistant
coaches and even the journalists who followed the trip of the
Catalan team to Scotland. Pep wanted to send a message to the
whole group. So it would stay in their memory.

The players were silently waiting for Pep to speak. While that
didn't happened, Pep made eye contact with the people present
and tried to understand who was more or less attentive. Some already knew him better, like Xavi, Iniesta, Messi, Piqué and Tito Vi-
lanova. It was then that Guardiola started:

> *"The team has been through a time when not everybody was as
> professional as they should have been. It is time for everybody to
> run and to give their all. I've been part of this club for many years
> and I am aware of the mistakes that have been made in the past,
> I will defend you to the death but I can also say that I will be very
> demanding of you all: just like I will be with myself."*

> *"I only ask this of you. I won't tell you off if you misplace a pass,
> or miss a header that costs us a goal, as long as I know you are
> giving 100 per cent. I could forgive you any mistake, but I won't
> forgive you if you don't give your heart and soul to Barcelona."*

> *"I'm not asking results of you, just performance. I won't accept
> people speculating about performance, if it's half-hearted or peo-
> ple aren't giving their all."*

"This is Barça, gentlemen, this is what is asked of us and this is what I will ask of you. You have to give your all. A player on his own is no one, he needs his team-mates and colleagues around him: every one of us in this room, the people around you."

"Many of you don't know me, so we will use the next few days to form the group, a family even. If anyone has any problems, I'm always available, not just in sporting matters but professional, family, environmental."

"We're here to help each other and make sure there is spiritual peace so that the players don't feel tension or division. We are one. We are not little groups because in all teams this is what ends up killing team spirit."

"The players in this room are very good, if we can't get them to win anything, it will be our fault. Let's stick together when times are hard. Make sure that nothing gets leaked to the press. I don't want anybody to fight a battle on his own."

"Let's be united, have faith in me. As a former player, I have been in your shoes; I know what you are going through, what you are feeling. The style comes dictated by the history of this club and we will be faithful to it. When we have the ball, we can't lose it. When that happens, run and get it back. That is it, basically."

When the talk ended the journalist felt that the people, the team and the group were seduced. When leaving the room, Xavi commented that all they needed to know had been said. That many talks could follow but that had been the key talk.

The truth is that Pep and Mourinho don't play but take a direct part in the game. Them and all the coaches. And their communication has an important weight in the actions of their athletes. We are most certainly going to watch the changes in the way the players will act when these two coaches start with their respective teams. And, without questioning the quality of those who left, those starting now have great quality and interacting methods, which are interesting and quite different from those previously used both in the United and the City.

As a rule a manager already takes an active part in the trainings and conferences, he leads the athletes, gesticulates, talks with the athletes individually or in group, points out, sets the example, and therefore we will probably have Mourinho, more than Guardiola, handling well the communication baton of those speaking and those listening.

It will also be interesting to watch if these two managers are going to change and which fields, in their way of communicating, are going to be altered. We should also add that in a team and at a match it is important to keep in mind that every behaviour is communication. Any behaviour or lack of it will result in a behaviour, which, if well interpreted, is a very important tool for those leading and also for the players within the teams. Mourinho e Guardiola, not as great managers but because they are in the first place great human resources managers, will put those changes into context.

Motivation: ways and processes

*"My motivation is what I consider to be the
engine that motivates others, even because
my motivation is directly connected with
others and their motivations."*

José Mourinho

*"I only ask this of you. I won't tell you off if you misplace
a pass, or miss a header that costs us a goal, as long
as I know you are giving 100 per cent. I could forgive
you any mistake, but I won't forgive you if you don't
give your heart and soul for the club."*

Pep Guardiola

Motivation is that theme that creates controversy among managers. Not only around the way they practice it, but also around the importance of it being stimulated by the manager or being a responsibility of the athletes. It is true that the best athletes are those tending to motivate for inherent causes. And here the coach is more a partner than a driver who has more skills to manipulate that motivation.

Although the manager is not responsible for everything that surrounds him and is part of the training and the competition, it is still the coach who has more impact in the satisfaction and meaning the athlete takes from his sports practice. Therefore it is many times possible to watch a manager get or improve performances in some athletes which they have never achieved with other coaches and vice-versa. Vítor Baía gives an approach to a simple aspect supporting the basis for any relationship between manager and player, but that sometimes is forgotten by the coach[19]:

> "Players like to feel they are important. And when people don't give them that importance, sooner or later there will be problems. With Mourinho the players feel important, because we were involved in the process, but it was a global involvement, including from the so called stars to the kids of the junior teams."

When there is a context that the coach cannot control, there is another training context and a group atmosphere, communicational habits that manage to create tuning and empathy channels with the athletes, which may improve a lot what the athlete is predisposed to give for the coach or the vision of the project.

If on one hand these are the athletes tending to have the best performances, on the other hand we can find everything within a football team and, amongst this set of players, there is a need to get them motivated one by one, there is a need to create something that will motivate them all, knowing beforehand that many times by motivating a player, another can lose his motivation due to the different consequences that the motivation creates in both players.

How does Guardiola motivate? He discloses the following:

> "Stories about people who overcome difficulties, human actions are extraordinary things. This is a good part of this job, because each opponent, each rival, each situation are different and you always need to find something special to say to them: 'Guys, today is important' because of this and that. Most of the times it isn't tactic at all."

Karanka, Assistant coach to Mourinho in Real Madrid stated that "Mourinho is able to convince everyone that no objective is un-

---

[19] Lourenço, L. (2010)

reachable". Beyond the impact of the statement, there is the detail of "everyone" but not on the same way. And this is another amazing area to research about these two football magicians and their leadership.

But Mourinho talks about his way to motivate. His beliefs about the process[20]:

> *"I think that the best way to motivate – at least what I find more consistent. Leaves less doubts, easier to understand and with longer durability – is to motivate others with my own motivations. I started like this and will end like this, I think that my own motivation is the best engine of the motivations of those I lead. That is, I want to win, I want to be the best, I want to gain the collective prizes, but also individual ones, I want to win titles after titles, I want to get the best contract, I want to earn more money, I want to better prepare my family's future, I want to be recognised as the best or one of the best, I want to leave my mark where I go, I want that the fans of the clubs where I worked remind me as someone important; these are some of my – many – motivations and that, in a natural way, I transmit, each day, each hour, in the way I talk, how I gesticulate, even in the way I stress all that work with me. Therefore, my motivation is what I consider to be the engine that motivates others, even because my motivation is directly connected with others and their motivations."*

While working at FC Porto, he had lost at home with the Greek Panathinaikos by 0-1 and, when the game ended, José Mourinho approached the coach of the Greek team and some of his players. One of them was the Portuguese midfielder Chainho who played for Panathinaikos, and Mourinho told him: "Tell your mates who are celebrating that this shit doesn't end here. We will go there and win!" As soon as he got back to his locker room he firmly stated: "I warned their coach, I warned their players that we are going to go there and win, and I said exactly the same to our supporters."[21]

---

[20] *Lourenço, L. (2010)*
[21] *Lourenço, L. (2010)*

Stankovic, his player at Inter Milan, shares an action that points out the skill of Mourinho to motivate and commit the players even more, by offering them some rest:

> *"When we won the first championship, three matches from the end, he came to me and said: Take your wife and go to Dubai for a week, you don't need to come to the training. You worked so much for me that you deserve seven days' rest. This gesture touched me."*

José Mourinho with these gestures, does not only reward or recognises, he commits. Much more. On the next season came another championship and another Champions League against Bayern at Barnabéu, where this player played an essential role. Some decades before, coach Wooden stated something like: "The coach is someone that can give instructions and correct without causing any grudge. The coach much search for opportunities to show he cares. These small gestures make the big difference." And there is no doubt that when we read Mourinho's statements, there is an endless set of confirmations that the Portuguese does understand the importance of these small gestures.

Alex Ferguson, on the ability of Mourinho to motivate, stated that:

> *"All his teams are motivated. All try to win, always. All have a method, a tactic. And all try to fulfil his scheme 100%. That means that he is able to easily motivate the teams."*

Within the motivation area, it is almost impossible to speak about a direct consequence of a manager's behaviour and the answer of his player. To do that we had to be inside the mind of each player and understand the real impact of the actions and words of their coaches. But an impact does exist!

The French striker, who was married when he was in London, the captain of Arsenal and one of the best scorers of Premier League, had a bit of a hard time in Catalonia. In Barça he wasn't none of that, he even got divorced. On the first half of the season with Guardiola, the performance of the striker was close to none. It is said that Pep invited him to dinner, and the striker answered with a hat-trick to Valencia on the next match, having finished the season with a score of 14 goals.

One of the ways José Mourinho has to motivate is to embody his teams, getting them involved, creating a feeling of commitment towards the behaviours which collectively are considered essential. José Mourinho tries to act in the group mentality and culture, being orderly, doing what he says and saying what he does, not accommodating with lack of discipline, raising the qualitative requirement pattern and the performance of the team. All this supported by a motivational flux that feeds, both psychologically and physically, on dedication, effort, and a rhythm of victories which, has the Portuguese says, are always the best support for the processes.

José Mourinho told Ideias & Negócios magazine that one of the big differences between managers is the motivation base:

> "(...) the difference stands on two points. One is to know how to coach – what not everyone knows how to do –, to know how to lead a team to get certain tactical behaviours on the field. The other point is motivation and beliefs."

There is a great connection here with the statement of the former player Jorge Costa: "What I really would like to know how to explain is how willing players are, myself included, to follow him to death". The Portuguese defender reinforces the commitment that Mourinho gets from his athletes and this, no matter what words we use, is the ability to commit to the goals, whatever they are, but that everyone consider as being their own!

Mike Kryzewski, or Coach K, considered to be one of the best basketball coaches, states about truth and motivation:

> "Truth is the basis for all we do. There is nothing more important than truth. In our team we always say the truth. We have to be honest with each other. There is no other way."

Coach K explains about motivation management that, during the season, the team must be managed by the coach with exuberance and excitement. That the coach must live that journey. And in the correct way. And all together. Sharing and always trying that the others always improve. And give a warning to any athlete that is not doing his share. And that you should hug and touch if needed. And we should be disappointed if those moments exist. Or enthusiastic with victories and good things. Never forgetting "it's all about the journey."

José Mourinho in an interview to Sport Life magazine states that the best way to coach the personality of the players is to win:

> "To win is the only thing that makes you have faith in what you do, that helps you build the group charisma which is the most important thing, not the personal charisma of each player. A coach's work is to unify the group character. When you manage that a team feels invincible, you have your path open to have a champion team." The Portuguese coach even shaved his hair to motivate his team: "I want to motivate the players of time to have a proper haircut".

What does this have to do with motivation? A lot. Motivation is tightly related with intrinsic and external values. Dozens of theories specially agree in one point: we all have different ways to self-motivate or being motivated and the context quite changes that impact. But the theories cross motivation against a clear definition of achievable goals. The information to know if they are indeed achievable comes from the truth of the information, of the source and of reality / view of those who search for the best definition of exciting goals.

As a matter of fact, the manager has a power over the athletes, which, many times, goes beyond the sports context, contributing to his motivation and not in line with other social and personal tasks. Unfortunately, many times the coach doesn't see it and even if he is paying attention, seldom measures his real power and intervention in an athlete's conscience and motivation. It is essential that he possesses this ability.

On an interview to Ideias & Negócios magazine while still working in FC Porto, the Portuguese stated:

"I say that for a team to be successful it has to be 100 per cent ready. And when I say 100 per cent, I am not able to separate what is physical from what is tactical, from what is psychological. For me a player is a whole (...) he practices under a concept we call "interconnection of all factors, where we work everything at once, including the motivational factor."

Considering that the motivational cycle starts with a need, it is necessary within the teams:

- To understand which are the individual needs and motivations that may jeopardize the group understanding and commitment;
- To make it a group need by means of group rules and processes that improve the group;
- To align the individual needs that fit perfectly with the group needs and the goals that leader intends to give to his work team.

Group motivation, as previously mentioned, involves a dynamic and combined process in which the motivation of one of the group members can take to the demotivation of another team member. If, on one hand, this makes the process rather interesting from the point of view of a challenge, and of commitment and dedication of the people involved, on the other hand it makes the whole process understandably more complex.[22]

Facilitating the whole motivational process is more effective if there is capture of signs so that the motivation can be more clear, and more objective and targeted. More than the motivation theories, like the need hierarchy of Maslow, Herzberg's theory, or Vroom's model, the application in teams is quite more complex since each person uses the tools which are more suitable for the team members, the contexts, and obstacles, and also has to know how to facilitate processes for motivation to happen and, above all, that it isn't a random episode.

---

[22] *Lança, R. (2012)*

One of the simplest methods that explain group motivation management is given by Blanchard[23] who claims for the teams the three C's model of performance and motivation:

- Cause: What makes performance happen;
- Conduct: Performance per se;
- Consequence: The reaction to performance.

How is all of this related to people and teams? Blanchard is one of the authors claiming that without consequences it is harder to change behaviours, since positive consequence can be 'enticing' and evidence that such a behaviour triggers something different and positive.

And how about teams? The positive consequence on the team – when understood – triggers enthusiasm, which if moderate and well managed increases trust in the processes through the results.

Motivation is one of the tools and one of the more complex and defying processes that a leader or a coach faces in his work. Combining and aligning individual goals with the group goals has several steps that need to be climbed in a sustainable way so that a wrong step doesn't bring down the small victories. Messi stated the following about the way Guardiola approaches the players:

> *"Pep immediately transmits an enormous pride on our work, trust and yearning for more. He earned our trust from day one because we could see things happening as a result of our work and that gave us a lot of trust".*

The journalist who best knows Pep Guardiola, Martí Perarnau, and had the chance to hang out with the manager several times and in different environments, says that Guardiola has a gift bigger than all the others. And it isn't to reinvent football. It is the active listening. "The great talent Pep has is to observe and listen

---

[23] *Blanchard, K. (2003).*

attentively. He is able to take in the working methods of other coaches like a sponge. He understands when he sees a good idea, steals it and then improves it". Ferran Adria, a friend of the coach and considered to be the Chef and mentor or El Bulli restaurant, one of the best in the world, says something similar: "Pep is not a creator, but an innovator".

Pep himself 'confirms' it:

> *"My knowledge is also inherited, it is not entirely mine, it belongs to all the coaches I have had in the past, some more than others, obviously, but all of them have taught me something." He also leaves us a reference about the requirement of managing to be better: "Mourinho made me a better coach."*

Emotional Intelligence and Talent

"I support work globalization, and not the separation of the physical, technical, tactical and psychological components, so the psychological side is essential."

José Mourinho

"Be yourself, be yourself, don't forget that!"

Pep Guardiola

Emotion is too important to be neglected. To be hidden. Luckily, coaches and leaders are giving increasingly more relevance to their feelings and the power that a good emotional management has to bring positive things to their daily lives and to enhance the human resources around them. To enhance what might be their emotional talent and develop the talent at several levels around it. António Damásio mentions this great discussion topic:

> *"Behaviour and mind, aware or not, and the brain itself that creates them, refuse to reveal feelings when emotion (and the several phenomena it hides) is not taken into account and isn't dully rewarded."*

Guardiola and Mourinho have talent. That is indisputable. And they have the rare talent of understanding and take advantage of the talent that surrounds them. Performing their work depends on these two talent variables, knowing beforehand that defining talent is something way more complex. Emotional intelligence also appears here in two different ways:

- The ability and need to know how to enhance and use the talent each person has in order to transform their knowledge into something practical, which can be an indicator of the so called practical intelligence;

- The ability and need to watch, to process and manage to evaluate the potential and talent of those surrounding them, and which are the talents they need to reach their goals, both individually and collectively.

The goalkeeper Victor Valdes said about Guardiola:

"Pep is the secret weapon of this group. If we put aside the quality of the players, he is the special talent of the group. Way beyond the rest of the team and technical staff. He is the most important member of this team".

To define talent implies to address the multiplicity and diversity of profiles, abilities and existing skills, since their meaning is so comprehensive and personalised as the number of people we are analysing. It can be stated that all people have talents, but those talents are not the same for everyone, existing different types of talents. Being that the performance of talent assumes different dimensions.

The talent is inherent to the human being and influences the individual at personal, relational and professional levels. The personal performance of talent has a direct impact on happiness, well-being, trust and motivation of individuals, being essential to each one's search of doing more and better. This level of performance, within the scope of the talent society, is the basis to develop social and professional dimensions.

Those managing human resources at this level, like these two managers, have to possess another type of intelligence. The practical intelligence, the ability to adapt to situations so that they can, as soon as possible, get back to a control zone of the several variables within the environment that surrounds them. In football jargon to always be on the game and above it!

The overall difference between emotion and feeling is easier than we might think. Emotions are actions together with ideas and ways of thinking, emotional feelings are, above all, perceptions of what our body does during the emotion, together with the perceptions of our states of mind during the same time period. António Damásio helps us to better understand what is going on in the mind of any person, especially in the mind of a leader who is responsible to manage other minds and enhance and understand other people's emotions.

Daniel Goleman, another author and researcher in the area of emotional intelligence, reinforces the idea that we must practice our behaviour;our emotions under pressure, and learn to enhance the emotions of the people we relate to and deal with on a daily basis by communicating in a more emotional way when needed. In the course of our lives we acquire some behavioural habits through education and training we are submitted to, mainly in what concerns quality and requirement of actions within the several learning contexts.

The scholar and neurosurgeon António Damásio, gives us a precious recommendation:

> "The fact that we can unchain any emotion in others and the other way around, testifies the powerful mechanism through which feelings flow from one person to another. To show our emotions is automatic and unconscious and, therefore, whenever we look to supress them, we are required a conscious and active effort seldom well succeeded."

When we watch the work of José Mourinho and Pep Guardiola, we understand that besides their work, they are constantly associated with high potential. That is, we always expect more. We are also demanding with these too football and leadership magicians. There are several studies to determine what makes someone a "talent", someone with "high potential". This definition, or better, assessment, is performed under different methods and criteria, according to the context of the assessment. Four factors keep coming up[24]:

- Ambition: To reach a high position implies almost every time to give in to the need of spending a lot of time to get results, work hard, focus, take time from your personal life, etc.
- Ability: Besides skills and abilities an individual should have, it is necessary to have the ability to keep on learning and adapting to new demands and new learnings coming from situations often quite different from the expected.
- Agility: Agility in this field means to make your mind responsive. Work and enhance curiosity, the discovery, to understand simplicity within complexity, alignment, to be responsive to commitment to your own development, help others, and also the agility of results, like flexible ideas, take on new situations and always work well in group.
- Performance/Focus: To lead ideas, projects or people, means to take advantage of personal fulfilment and of the task during the journey of wanting to reach something, either the best idea or to obtain be largest collective intelligence possible.

Inside what can be considered a football match there are many games and the need for several talents! Some more visible, others more implicit. And there are games for the teams, players, coaches, managers, and so on. The coaches have their own games, besides the technical, tactical and organizational issues. Besides coaching. Communication is becoming more of an intra- and interpersonal game. And their emotions and what these can change and enhance in others.

[24] Ulrich, D & Smallwood, N. (2012). "What is talent?". *Leader to Leader*, *63*, 55-61.

Coaches don't seem to be able to resist much being quiet in what concerns the communicational and emotional management of their team and the attempt to condition the other team. They seem to be so unable to resist these games like the athletes are not to pull the opponents shirt. A sort of vice, in which coaches try to have a set of tools to, also here, be winners!

"I already felt several times that I have changed the opponents' behaviour withy what I say. It doesn't happen with all, but it does happen many times. Therefore I have no doubts that it is a path to explore". This is a sentence of José Mourinho. Possibly the theme of emotional intelligence concerning the Portuguese manager could end here. But it is even more captivating to understand how he does it. And the reaction of those who feel it. Like the time Mourinho not only disclosed the eleven members of his team but also, one by one, the players that the manager of Barcelona at the time, the Dutch Frank Rijkaard, would call to play.

Alex Ferguson has an excellent sentence that, although being directed to Mourinho, would also fit Guardiola perfectly: "I admire people that show us their emotions. They show that they are of importance to them."

Still about the Portuguese, in spite of the first small misunderstandings, he leaks the following in his autobiography:

> "Everyone I talk to tells me that José deals extremely well with the players. He's meticulous with his planning, worries about details. When we get to know him, he becomes a pleasant person, and he manages to make fun of himself, tell jokes about himself."

And balances, in a very effective way, his emotions with all the knowledge and the goals he wants to reach:

> "There is no doubt that José is pragmatic. The basic principle of his system is to assure that his team does not lose. If you put five, he puts six. If you put six, he puts seven."

On the other hand, Guardiola always tries to put aside the idea that what he obtains comes from his talent or the guaranteed knowledge of the game or the training. Guardiola doesn't think of himself like having talent or being a genius. "Just a man with ideas. And he steals them from others and makes them better." This information contains a lot of emotional intelligence, an attempt that players with talent don't get the idea that they are ahead of those less talented. And if there are managers who work with talents, Guardiola is one of them. As well as Mourinho of course!

Not willing to develop much the intelligence theme, the Italian defender Franco Baresi stated: "Pep was already very intelligent as a player. I always thought that whenever I faced him on the field. He knew how to move and was way ahead of the other players." Alex Ferguson, after his defeat on the Champions League in 2011 against Guardiola's Barcelona, commented: "In all my coaching career, this is the best team I played against".

But things are not always easy. Sometimes, some more than others, people fail in using their emotions according to their goals. To think about the reason that lead Mourinho to be unsuccessful on his last season at Chelsea is aiming at possible targets. It isn't normal that a champion, at the drop of a hat, in a year where he reinforces his squad, not being an outsider – as was the case of Leicester –, just lowers his performance, both qualitatively and quantitatively.

Of course that one of the targets that could explain this sudden change was the Eva Carneiro affair. No one ever knew for certain which was the event after the game that triggered everything. But here are the words of the Portuguese coach, who seldom talked about this subject: "Fearn and Eva won't be at the bench on Sunday, but that doesn't mean they won't be there in the future." They weren't and they never were and it is assumed that this is one of the few times Mourinho failed. Not in the game strategy, nor the tactics, but in what concerns media hype and impact that the event caused. But like the German tennis player Steffi Graf would say: "You can never measure your success if you never failed". And for sure this less positive experience will bring something good for the next season in England.

But Mourinho has been giving several examples of how he manages to overcome really difficult moments. His goalkeeper Dudek of Real Madrid shared what happened after the 0-5 defeat against Barcelona. The Polish confided the moment immediately after the game:

> "5-0. Can you believe it? Barcelona defeated us by 5-0. It was a massacre. After the game our locker room was a chaos. Some were crying, others were fighting, and others didn't take their eyes of the floor. Then José Mourinho entered the locker room. He knew it had been really bad. He looked at us and said:

> "I know it hurts. A lot. For many of you, this may seem like the biggest defeat of your lives. But it's just the beginning. They are happy now, as if they already won the championship. But they just won a match. There is still a long way to go to win the title. Tomorrow you will have the day off. But you are not going to stay at home. I want you to get your wives, kids or friends and take a tour around town. I want you to show people that you know how you deal with this. You might listen to bad things on the way, but don't hide. Show your courage. And after, we will fight for the title."

> I thought to myself: 'Damn, this makes sense'. Everyone looked at each other and thought this had worked. We ended up getting back on our feet faster than anyone would think. At that moment, after what Mourinho said, I understood the real importance of the psychological side in sports. How it can quickly make you win or lose. I also understood how intelligent and psychologically strong Mourinho is."

The midfielder Deco said about Mourinho:

> "What affected me the most was the psychological control he had over all the players. He knew exactly how to act with each of the players. He also knew that sometimes he had to be tough with a few and knew exactly how that would reflect in the game. He also

knew how he could, indirectly, give some "power" to the player to discuss with him the game tactics, but without losing authority, and at the same time keeping the morals high of the football player at home, because he knew that the player needed that kind of encouragement. So, what I think was fantastic was that control, that perception of knowing how far he could go with any of the players and how, therefore, he could get the maximum perform-ance from them. And I am not talking technically or tactically, but psychologically. In that field he knew exactly how to get the better of each one."

Still according to the Luso-Brazilian midfielder: "In the locker room Mourinho is quite relaxed, but, when he starts talking to the press, he likes to entangle things, he is playing a role." On the other hand, Thiago Alcântara thinks Guardiola is amazing in tac-tical terms but "(...) he is even better in psychological terms, al-though sometimes he is so intense it can be exhausting". This detail is becoming more important and it is interesting to under-stand how and when it is pointed out by his players.

According to the self-determination theory (SDT)[25], the three basic psychological needs in all cultures, innate and during the several development stages, are ability (when an individual has the op-portunity to set goals and show his abilities), degree of related-ness with the other individual or with the task, and autonomy (when we act according to our interests and values).

Analysing the last years of Mourinho and Guardiola it is possible to identify situations where each of these leadership magicians managed to enhance their squads needs, in different ways ac-cording to the situations, contexts and players, for a higher degree of relatedness of some players with their tasks, and the ability to recognise which athletes needed more freedom and others more comfort, so that they felt protected by control or the permanent inclusion of the players in the common goals of their teams. And where the individual goals should be included.

---

[25] *Ryan, R.M. (1985) in Lança, R. & Lopes, M. P. (2015)*

One of the biggest merits of both Mourinho and Guardiola is that they always understand, from the moment they embrace a challenge, that all players have different personalities, turning themselves into perfect conflict managers. This led to Mourinho already speaking Italian when he arrived to Italy, and Guardiola introducing himself in German during his presentation in Munich. Did it allow a better communication? Of course. But to whom? Not to those speaking, since for Mourinho and Guardiola it would probably be more comfortable to communicate in Portuguese and Spanish. Or in English for both.

This concern about the others, to show they were already some steps ahead of what was expected, is the ability to perceive what could cause a good impression on others. What could cause impact! And we are not just talking about knowing which players they would have, who would do this better or if they have to work more this or that. Probably with the amount of football managers consume, they would already know a lot about the athletes of both teams, even if they were never to coach at City or United. But this detail, well thought of, made the media, the fans, and the players to think about their professionalism and the level of demand, which was about to arrive to their teams!

And it shows in the way they prepare everything. Always concerned about the others. About what the athlete might feel or hear so that they can reach his emotions! Rui Faria, the loyal assistant coach of Mourinho, states that "Coaching on the edge requires a mentality of coaching on the edge. Therefore the mentality comes before the action." Still on this subject, José Mourinho states that "when I prepare a training session, I prepare a global activity, never forgetting its implications at different levels".

Pep had the same opinion and, when in Bayern Munich, he stated it building the bridge between practice and the match:

> *"You play at the rhythm you practice. In a match the player can slow down the rhythm according to how he faces tactically or technically a move, but as a group, the rhythm of the team relies a lot on the way you practice. If you practice like crazy, you will play the same way. And these men practice like crazy."*

Rui Faria, using José Mourinho's words about the quality and usefulness of his assistant in his teams, tells to the newspaper "O Jogo" what a practice should be, with all the pillars inherent to the athletes:

> "The final goal is to play. And, if that is the goal, practice can only have one meaning: make them play. If the goal is to improve the game and the quality of the organization, those parameters can only be substantiated through practice situations or exercises where that organization can be worked on."

Bill Walsh, one of the biggest coaches of American football, states that the mind of a coach must be able to work in an effective way and decide even under the most stressing situations one can imagine, and that in these cases they must be able to show an outstanding ability to separate guilt, responsibilities and attacks:

> "The mind of a coach can never bring down the game to blaming the players for the success or failure, it has to overcome that temptation."

The striker Zlatan Ibrahimovic had the opportunity to play for several big clubs. And in those clubs he also had the opportunity to be coached by several good managers, among which José and Pep. For the Swedish, Mourinho is a coach who likes to instil a lot of discipline in his athletes through mental games. The striker blurt out that the coach likes to use the same match scheme, as long as it keeps resulting positively, and that Mourinho, when preparing the matches, had the ability to get into the athletes' minds. He even stated that: "[I] invested a lot of adrenaline playing for him. Nothing was ever good. José Mourinho knows how to treat a player."

About Pep, with whom he had some disagreements when playing for Barcelona, the Swedish revealed that Pep likes to motivate his players to always go further, even if the team is already winning by a considerable advantage. Ibra also pointed out the intelligence of the coach to evaluate the opponents:

"I had Guardiola as a coach, the big brain of football. He had solutions for each team we faced, knowing exactly what we needed to do to win and exactly how he wanted us to achieve that".

But about his experience with Pep in Barcelona, Ibra scored one of those integrity goals when he claimed:

"I know how to separate things. Barcelona is the best team in the world. I knew it when I came here and when I left. Guardiola is an amazing coach; the problems between us are something different."

It is understood that emotional intelligence helps a leader to achieve more sustainable processes to lead his team, thus also helping to create more long lasting processes. How? That would be for sure what Mourinho and Guardiola put into practice. And us? Well, we will watch, step by step, to understand, learn and perceive that in this area there isn't just one way, but some ways are more correct than others.

Coaches must be aware and know how to interpret their emotions and their consequences, so that they can have a better and faster understanding of what they can trigger in others. Once again, to know the causes of a result is quite different from knowing the final result.

The Catalan journalist, Marti Peramau, gives us an inside perspective of someone who was around the Catalan manager and his athletes. Peramau comments that Guardiola:

"Is not a tough man and doesn't mind admitting it or show it. If he is worried about something, he scratches is head. If he is pleased with a training session, he yells, applauds and kisses people. If he is not pleased, he steps out and sits on a corner. He shows his emotions with no filters. He's convinced that you have to react optimistically when you lose. But he is no super hero, he is just an ordinary person, who doesn't mind crying in front of his players when taken by emotion, or laugh like a child."

Empathy, highly associated with the emotional intelligence, gives the leader the ability of being more flexible, of adapting to more people and with less discomfort zones, due to having to put himself in other people's shoes. To have and to get a better emotional control allows him to know his faults and take more advantage of emotions under situations where emotions can or should overcome less rational decisions and vice versa.

It allows a better and more reliable understanding of others, like knowing what could be beneficial to develop and improve the skills of the team members. In a team, emotional intelligence allows to solve and manage better the emotions of others, to manage conflicts in a more effective way and to congregate individual goals and encourage a more global commitment.

The self-conscience and self-discipline that Mourinho and Pep so many times proclaim and mention in their exercises of rhetoric and work philosophy, allow them to be more humble and assertive to recognise and assume his weaknesses and strengths in managing and leading a team. To be aware of the strengths increases one's confidence levels as long as they are channelled to a search for better results and not to hide weaknesses.

Finally, all this comes together in the ability of generating a bigger and better impact on the people being led. This does not mean that emotional intelligence and its components are the only important variant. Technical abilities are relevant too and are the precondition to reach some top positions.

Their teams and their tribes

"The team I wish for is the one where, at a certain moment, facing a certain situation, all players think the same. That is my concept of a team. This is only possible with time, work and tranquillity."

José Mourinho

"In football, things don't happen because players do or don't do what I tell them. No, football is way more complicated than all that."

Pep Guardiola

"Gentlemen, good morning. You can imagine what a huge motivation it is for me to be here, to coach this team. It is the ultimate honour. Above all, I love the club. I would never make a decision that would harm or go against the club. Everything I am going to do is based on my love for FC Barcelona. We need and want order and discipline." This was the Guardiola's presentation speech. Where he defines how he is. A vision, a lot of passion. To set high standards. In terms of feelings and rising to the moment. And two requirements. Group norms and rules.

A career as manager is not easy. It has as much of excitement as it has of difficulty. And curiously, when we start analysing parts of football history, of Mourinho's and Guardiola's lives, there are episodes that end up leaving a feeling of ambiguity, because although some actions were taken in a spontaneous way, considering the change of contexts and of clubs, managers are forced to portrait themselves in a very sublime manner.

We will understand much better the reality of being a football coach, if we first understand the reality of being a coach of any kind of sports, because there will be more things in common than differentiating. Vince Lombardi, as a group reference, speaks about the profession and of wanting to be a leader:

> "Leaders aren't born, they are built. And they are built like anything else: with hard work. And that is the price to pay for that goal or any other goal."

And that is also what makes this field of leadership analys is fantastic. The need to know that things are under control but that control, that organization and group intelligence depends on the ability to work and observe every day, being attentive to much more than just technical, tactical and physical skills of the athletes.

Using the ordinary sentence that a team is more than the sum of its parts, in procedural and cognitive terms, the questions remaining for those who work teams should be:

- Which are the processes and the properties of teams? And how should these be different from the processes and properties of those composing the whole?
- How is the cognition of teams changed by the existence of more or less group skills?[26]

Luckily sport teams have the biggest and best common denominators of what is needed for a team to work. In some way there must be a very strong reason for us to work as a team instead of just adding up individual efforts, which, as valuable as they may be, always fall short of what a team may achieve. But unfortunately, and managers know it well, the individualities are not enough, no matter how skilled or talented.

---

[26] *Eccles, D. W. & Tenenbaum, G. (2004)*

Research and several works on these always exciting subjects show and reinforce that the factors affecting group properties and procedures for the team to be more than the sum of the parts are the following:

- Group coordination
- Communication
- Organization

Coordination of teams involves the integration of tasks, people, rules, and satisfaction, among other factors. One of the most investigated factors is the number of athletes per team. Too many members may spoil the coordination, cohesion and communication itself. It is no coincidence that coaches take very seriously the number of athletes in their squads. Not only for budget reasons, but because they know that in the future it will bring motivational issues, discontent and poor productivity. And that is a problem for the team and the coaches!

As for the group communication, as already seen in the José Mourinho's and Pep Guardiola's examples, it is essential for the teams. When talking about team leadership and personal interactions that build among the members, we have to be aware that each and every behaviour is communication. Any behaviour or lack of it will trigger another behaviour or lack of response, being constantly generating signs after signs, which when well interpreted are very important tools for those managing, leading and also for the athletes.

The ideal situation would be to accomplish what Mike Kryzewski says: "Communication must be thought and practiced so that it can be carried out as one", even because group communication many times occurs in a very unnatural way. As expressed by the author Johann Wolfgang Goethe, the commitment of every player, and accomplishing that commitment collectively, has always been one of the main challenges for every manager, no matter who they are:

"Until we commit there is hesitation, possibility to go back. In what concerns all actions of initiative (and creation) there is an elementary truth, and ignoring it kills a large number of splendid ideas and plans: the moment we commit, Providence also moves a step ahead. Then there are facts occurring that help us to reach the purpose, facts that without that commitment wouldn't have existed. A chain of events born from our decision generates into our favour a whole sort of unforeseen incidents and encounters, a material assistance that no man has ever dreamt would come to his help. Start right now what you think or dream you can do."

The following paragraph by José Mourinho about his opponent at the time, Barcelona coached by Guardiola, shows how important vision, alignment, and team culture are:

"Barcelona has a philosophy since the Cruyff, even since Michels. Then Van Gaal arrives, an upgrade. Now Pep arrives, a more consistent upgrade due to the understanding Pep has of this culture, but it is an upgrade work. Real Madrid is a work of contradictions. A contradiction of ideas from different coaches that keep coming, instead of an upgrade to improve those ideas."

The leadership of a coach starts with the reason for coaches to lead: their teams! José Mourinho defends his teams. A lot! Indeed it is interesting to see his ability to rapidly change shirts. One time when he was in London working for Chelsea he stated that: "The circumstances are hard for us with the new football rules we have to face. It is not possible to have penalties against Manchester United. It's not conspiracy, it is a fact." Let's wait for the new chapters. Let's move on!

José Mourinho states that one of the best advices he got from Bobby about managing teams and players was:

"When you win, you shouldn't assume you are the team, and when you lose, you shouldn't think you are rubbish."

This meaning that a leader should not claim the victory of the team as his, nor as his failure in case of defeat. It is important that managers are able to learn that the whole team should have the credits for winning as well as the responsibility for losing.

The Portuguese manager has this common denominator. That is voicing these statements and, after a couple of days, he retracts so that he doesn't have to apologise, but always contextualizing his statements and coming up clean. An amazing ability. Xabi Alonso had the chance (and luck) of being trained by the two coaches. About Mourinho he said: "Each coach has his method and Mourinho has a very special idea about group work. Unity favours the common good and is the best way to get positive results."

Pep Guardiola also stands strong by his teams. Indeed it is impossible for a manager not to defend his work group. Possibly this point comes up as an important factor in the success of a manager. The way he does it is possibly an indicator of success or not. Some say that Mourinho shoots to the head of his players and Guardiola to the heart. This could be a way to interpret their actions or words, but judging from the diversity of athletes they have coached, it would be impossible to always shoot to the head or to the heart and be successful.

Pep describes himself well, as it happened during his presentation on his first day of work before the journalists, stating that he values the players who are good mates. And with these statements he proves what we have been pointing out in the previous chapters, that Guardiola places his bet in a management with a human component:

> "I like the players who believe in themselves and in the team. I don't want any player who thinks he can be the whole team, but one who helps the club. My tactic applies to the quality of the players. I don't ask for anything they can't give."

There are no recipes for how the managers get the values and indexes they want from their teams. Just the notion that some group behaviours are essential and that, without them, individual skills are most of the times of no use. The manager Alex Ferguson states exactly that:

"In my line of work, cohesion is not just a nice concept you use or trash as you feel. Without it, you can't achieve anything. Selfishness, partisanship, internal division kill a team. As a coach I was never interested to produce a set of brilliant individuals. There is no way you can replace talent but, on the field, talent without common goals has no value."

Trust and being authentic are usually two of the group rules in high performance teams. About these two skills Pep says:

"I judge my players for their work, not for their private life. I am not the police. I am in bed at 10 pm and have no intention of getting up and check if my players are in bed. This is why most of the times we stay at home, instead of going to a Hotel where there is more control".

This liability delegation from Guardiola has a lot to do with the Spanish tradition and contextualization. He explained the difference between the Spanish habits and the German:

"People in Spain are not used to stay the day before at a Hotel. But if they don't rest, they won't be at their best level and thus will play worse. They can lose their jobs if they do."

But Guardiola also has rules or norms for what he wants. Mourinho has them too. Indeed it is safe to say that any manager and his game and team philosophy apply to a certain athlete profile. The Catalan coach talking to the coach of sub-19 from Azerbaijan, Patrícia González, states his preference for a certain type of player:

"Patrícia, I'm going to give you some advice: always choose the best. Always! Who are the best players? Are they those getting the most attention from the media? No! The best players are those who never let go of the ball. Who always know when to make a pass and know when they cannot lose it at all. These are the best. And these are the ones you always have to use, even they have a more quiet profile than the others."

The tribes and the way the coaches manage to "close" their teams into a group alignment and a lot of commitment is one of the best kept! At this level you cannot lose your nerve. These two leadership magicians gave us, give us and will for sure continue to give us episodes that teach us something. Mourinho even stated that he "preferred to play with 10 players only than wait for a player who is late for the bus" or "The players are not the stars, the team is."The Ivorian Drogba stated several times that Mourinho didn't teach him how to play football: "He taught me to play in a team, which is something different."

The Spanish sports journal As reproduced some time ago the 10 commandments of José Mourinho:

1. The players are not the stars, the only star is the team
2. The guilt belongs to the coach, the liability belongs to all
3. It is totally forbidden to self-exclude
4. Punctuality is sacred
5. The hotel is like a bunker
6. You can only drink water in the rooms
7. Mobile phones are forbidden
8. Everyone is equally important
9. Each player gets a personalized DVD with the characteristics of the opponent he will face within his range
10. The team works hard to win the matches

Drogba about the first time of Mourinho in Chelsea said the following:

> "He's very protective. He's a person who provides the maximum protection to his working group, he considers as family. Therefore he speaks a lot on the first person to protect the group."[27]

On the other hand when Guardiola was asked if he thought Messi was the world's best player, he answered "I don't see or discuss things like that. I don't analyse the player alone, I try to under-

---

[27] Lourenço, L. (2010)

stand him within the general scope of the team."even having later claimed, in other situations when he was Barcelona's coach, that Messi was above all the others.

In one of his most famous sentences, the Portuguese coach, José Mourinho, stated about the type of players he liked to have on the team:

> *"All we need is a strong group of players and not a Hollywood star. But what the hell are the galactic? Their image comes from their social life and the fame as players ends up being an add-on. I suspect that type of galactic. My suspicion falls not on their ability as football players, but on the fact that the environment surrounding them might come to influence their exhibitions."[28]*

Following the careers of these two coaches (and others who reached this level) we understand that they are always on duty. In the slightest details, they are there. In a slight comment, in a more implicit message, one could say they don't sleep. And they don't sleep precisely because they defend their teams and placed in the most suitable position for the coming challenges. Even if there is avian flu, like it happened when Mourinho was in the Chelsea and diverted the attention from a close score of Manchester United with a current issue which was the avian flu, and the possibility of a swan to die in Scotland. The captain of the blues, John Terry, commented on this event: "In the locker room we thought how he mastered taking the pressure out of the players, it's amazing."

Mourinho states and defends one of his beliefs which he frequently mentions in his talks[29]:

> *"The strongest thing a team may have is to play as a team. More important than having one or too great players, it is playing as a team. For me this is very clear: the best team is not the one with the best players, but the one that plays as a team. To play as a team is being organized, is to have some regularities that make*

---

[28] Lança, R. (2012)

[29] Amieiro, N.; Barreto, R.; Oliveira, B. & Resende, N. (2006).

the players, in the four moments of the game, to think the same at the same time. But that is only possible with time, work and tranquillity. Because one thing is the players understanding and trying to do what I want, the other is to being able to do it as a team. That takes time."

Knowing beforehand that the members of the team are different from each other, with a personal identity side (education, religion, values, beliefs, etc.) and a social side(training, academic life, professional experience, etc.), and they are constantly interacting, to combine people towards a common goal is a quite demanding task.

We stress out, however, that this can be as demanding as it is exciting. To discover, not only how, but also why the same teams are able to reach levels of performance so different from each other, and even more amazing, to show different performances within different contexts or with different leaders. The complexity of high performance teams is like multiplying the complexity and the highly developed mental models that individuals with high performances generally have in some areas. Trust plus the ability to interact and align mental maps of the several members of the team Is a game with a hard to get victory. And as is usually said, it is not the victory and the stage of being the best which is hard to achieve, but the hardest is to stay there.[30]

Team leadership is as theme as exciting as it is complex. Besides the complexity existing in the members of a team, there is the group complexity which is not the sum of the individualities. The contexts, the states of mind, the restrains, all this requires continuous changes from those who lead and those who are led, against the risk of not being able to control or take advantage due to the lack of capacity of keeping up with changes.

---

[30] *Lança, R. (2012)*

The teams, as a system, present three principles like any other system:

- Full scope: A system is a set of elements interacting and not the count of the number of elements in the system. The characteristics of the team don't have to be the same characteristics of its members, since the team has its own specific dynamics and has to be understood as such.
- Homeostasis: All systems tend to preserve at all costs their initial state of balance, reacting to internal or external mutations with answers that try to re-establish that balance. May be the most amazing characteristic, and that totally depicts nowadays teams and people, is the resistance to change, which happens even when the change is needed and can bring advantages to the team.
- Circularity: All and each change in one of the members causes a change in all the others and the interaction with the system causes a retroaction which cannot be 100 per cent previewed.

These three principles can be explained with examples from a football team trained by one of the managers discussed here. The so called Barça formula, coached by Pep Guardiola:

- This formula of outnumbering doesn't guarantee anything, because in the end all, everything depends on skill, precision, and concentration of the artists to assure the advantage of space and to take the best decisions, to always have a player alone or not marked by the opponent, a secure line that can be used to make the pass. In this sense, football became all about the ball and spaces.
- Words of Pep himself: *"The players need to know that they don't have to be afraid of losing the ball, because football is really that. Messi knows that he can always try his movements because he is aware of having team players behind to help him if needed. When all the strikers and defenders feel like they are important, we know we have a winning team."*
- *"The right attitude is the most important when we defend. We can talk about a thousand concepts but what keeps a team together, what helps the athletes to defend or attack is the attitude. If you want, you can run for your mate because you will be making him improve, but this is not about him improving but yet about your own improvement."*

It is relevant to develop a holistic image of team management regardless of the characteristics it might present or tries to consolidate. The high performance teams or those that occasionally reach success show an almost universal characteristic: the ability their leader has to know all the members and of the identity he intends to build or that the team already has when he starts his job.

And Mourinho is an expert in building high performance teams, from União de Leiria to Chelsea. To instil the so needed competitive spirit and create empathy with his players. And like the author Daniel Pink stated: "Empathy makes us human". And Mourinho has an amazing ability to make his athletes let go of their personal goals and raise the bar with an individual and group goal:

"I am a team coach and I usually say that first I don't teach my players to play football, I teach them to play as a team. Then as second goal, I always want the whole to be more than the sum of the parts, therefore, and I repeat, I am a "team coach". But I don't forget that I am working with individuals, human beings. And each player is a different man, each with their own personality, their way of being and way of life, even with a different body, and because of that, I also need to look at them and work with them individually, so that I can have the maximum effectiveness to promote the whole/team."[31]

Vince Lombardi, mythical coach of American football, pointed out the relationship between a good team spirit and success:

"The difference between mediocrity and greatness is the feeling the players have for each other. Most people call it team spirit. When the players are imbued with that special feeling, you know you've got yourself a winning team."

The team management and leadership provide daily, and in a fast way, signs and behaviours that have to be perceived and collected by those leading. It is not easy and no one said it would be, but the ability some leaders have to anticipate signs, behaviours, situations, failures, understanding them and relating them, makes them able to deal in a more balanced way with the characteristics of their team. To Pep Guardiola:

"The players are my main concern" and *"The only thing that matters in our game happens in the pitch. Nothing else matters."*

This follow-up and continuous evaluation may and should be perfected. Look at the sport teams and what they can teach us:

- In almost all team sports, those who start to win have more chances to win. What does this tell us? Facilitate the creation of group procedures that can be used as motivation, immediately on the first team tasks.
- Train, practice, repeat and progress. What does this tell us? Give space and time to fail, to perfect tasks, commu-

---

[31] *Lourenço, L. (2010)*

nicational processes, team procedures, to improve individual and group actions.

- Set aside time in the middle of the projects. Ask for time-out! What does this tell us? Having planned a break to think makes the moments to be dominated by the leader and by the team and not always imposed by the surrounding environment.
- Only change members of the team when you are sure that those leaving will be replaced in a qualitative way and that it won't change the balance of the team. What does this tell us? Teams that keep untouched, improve group actions, cooperation, and flexibility.

We leave here a definition that depicts the expression "collective intelligence" with much of what has been already mentioned and with the evidence given by these two excellent coaches that there are key pieces in this complex puzzle of managing people in highly competitive environments:

Collective Intelligence

It is the set of skills of the elements that compose the WHOLE and of the processes/dynamics created to enhance the value of EVERY human resources in accomplishing the proposed and aligned goals.

Teams make a positive difference through sustainable procedures which daily encourage, create, feed and impose their group identity. Some skills must be present, and throughout the book we managed to give several examples of how Pep Guardiola and José Mourinho work and encourage them:

- Ability to support one another
- Strong trust at a technical and personal level
- Straightforward and continuous/aligned communication
- Tolerance towards difference and none towards error
- Individual and group commitment

- Common goals
- Compatibility / alignment of wills, values, directions
- Cooperation
- Ability to adapt
- Excitement / Emotion / Openness
- Unselfishness

In the book 'Mourinho, Porquê tantas vitórias'[32] the method and terms of the guided discovery are analysed. The focus that should be given to the process, learning through practice, failure vs. success, individual and team reflexion. It contains an excerpt of the manager that makes it easier to understand how that guided tour is made:

> *"It isn't easy to go from theory to practice, mainly with top players, who don't accept what they are told just because of the authority of who tells them. You have to prove to them we are right. With me, tactical work isn't only a work with the sender on one side and the receiver on the other. I call it "guided discovery", this means that the players find out things from clues I give to them. For that I build practice situations that lead them to a certain path. They start to feel it, we talk, discuss and come to conclusions."*

And what about the need of an athlete and a coach to train those skills? There is a great need. "A great pianist does not run around the piano nor does he do push-ups on his fingertips. To be great he plays the piano. And being a great player is not running, doing push-ups or exercise in general. The best way to become a great football player is by playing football." This sentence is from José Mourinho and takes us to the need of working on our skills, actions, steps, attitudes which are needed to compete. We have to be prepared for that. Hence we have to play, practice, execute, and repeat.

Here it adds another very important theme, the conscious practice, a theory of Ericsson, Krampe e Tesch-Homer (1993) that claims a structured practice aiming to progress and improve performance, thus focusing in what it is really needed to improve performance.

---

[32] *Amieiro, N.; Barreto, R.; Oliveira, B. & Resende, N. (2006)*

These coaches are always questioned about the coaching of a group of several talents. Guardiola e Mourinho, top of the tops coach and relate daily with also top players. The way each piece fits the total puzzle and the type of impact that this piece/player causes in the group is one of the main concerns of these coaches. Sometimes there are talents that have what it takes to add individual and group qualities to the process and the results but, as time goes by, might not provide those needed qualities.

Mourinho is more aggressive in the competition. His players usually make fiercer teams and also reflect the way they act before other teams and players and sometimes it generates some conflicts. However, Mourinho always protects his players and his teams against external attacks.

Premier League and Manchester, a league and a city with even more charm

"The circumstances are hard for us with the new football rules we will have to face. It is not possible to have penalties against Manchester United. There is no conspiracy, it is a fact."

José Mourinho (when he was coaching for Chelsea)

"At the beginning of that month, it was announced I was leaving and that another manager had been hired. This affected the players and, to me, the two defeats we had at that time didn't allow us to be competing for the title."

Pellegrini on Guardiola

The Premier League is probably the most amazing and followed League in the world. It is a synchrony and symphony of good feelings which culminates in magic for those who like football, sports, fair play, and the way the teams and fans mix in a togetherness that in some cases looks like a rare event. A unique event inside another grand event.

Besides the existing magnificence, the 2016-17 season will have a set of coaches who became famous in other European leagues and who, little by little, we wished they all would confront in a single national league and not only on the Champions League. Pep Guardiola, Antonio Conte and, again, José Mourinho will join this season the excellent set of coaches already in the Premier League working in the British Islands, like Jurgen Klopp, Arsene Wenger, Claudio Ranieri, Mauricio Pochettino, Slaven Bilic, or Ronald Koeman.

On May 24, 2016 it was confirmed that the Portuguese would go to Manchester United and two great managers would come together in one single town. Although it was just the confirmation of what was expected, the next Premier League season will be exciting with all the excellent managers and for sure there will be shows inside and outside of the pitch.

The Portuguese arrives to Manchester without the aura he had the first time he arrived to England. And especially to a club whose supporters are not going to welcome him. Although the Dutch Van Gaal had a not very pleasant season, the truth is he recovered some mystique from training and had as assistant coach Ryan Giggs, who gathered the agreement of some to be the next coach for the 2016/17 season. Van Gaal even referred to Mourinho as being "an arrogant young man, who has no respect for authority".

The Welsh Giggs ended up being removed from the club, a decision that Alex Ferguson understood. The Scotch explained that a manager needs someone he can trust by his side, referring that this person is the Portuguese Rui Faria:

> "You have got to have, in your assistant, someone you have trusted all your life. When I came to United, I brought Archie Knox because he was a valuable person for me. I trusted him 100 per cent. Jose Mourinho has had his assistant for years and, quite rightly, has stuck by his own man. If Jose hadn't had an assistant, I know he would have taken Ryan."

On this subject, Mourinho stated that he understood the attitude and actions of all the parts involved:

> *"It is not his responsibility that he is not in the club, nor is it my fault. Ryan wanted to be Manchester United manager. And the board, the owners decided that the job was for me. 16 years ago I had to make the same decision and Ryan made his now. If he could be my assistant? He could be whatever he wanted, but he made his decision."*

This will be an emotional Premier League for sure. With several candidates, way beyond the two Manchester teams. Mourinho believes it too:

> *"My experience does not allow me to be naive. I was in Spain for two years, where the champion would be me or him [Guardiola]. There, the individual fights made more sense. In England, if we were to only focus on him and me, and City and United, there would be another team to become champions".*

And he goes on basing his comments on the existing competition that pleases so much those following the English championship:

> *"You look at the German championship and the last five years the same team won four times; in France, in four [PSG] won four. In Spain, Atletico won once and Barcelona the other three. In England, the last four years there have been four different champions. This says a lot about competitiveness. The fact that it has, perhaps, the most impactful TV rights in the game. The fact is that the television revenues are distributed in the way that allows the growth of the League as a competition, unlike other leagues where the sharks are always sharks. In England is quite the opposite."*

Therefore he assumed that speaking about a team, a manager, an enemy, although he doesn't like that word related to football, is not right in this country. In Spain he did it because "there were two horses running, there this kind of approach made sense, here it doesn't."

José Mourinho will continue his path of references, some more direct than others:

"There are managers that the last time they won a title was 10 years ago, others never. Mine was one year ago, if I have a lot to prove, imagine the others. It has never been important to me, I play against me, it is the feeling I have several times, I have to prove my quality to myself not to the others. I could have a defence approach to this job, but I can't, it is against my nature."

"The menu has to change for better and not for worse, and Manchester United was used to routine victories. We have to do better and better is not being fourth. I am 53 years old, maybe I am sick of myself, for having started so early. I am in trouble, but I was in more trouble the last five months, after the second it was a complete disaster."

The Portuguese always felt good in England, has he admitted three years ago when he was in Madrid: "I know that I am wanted in England, by the fans, by the media." The Portuguese manager considers that he is "already part of the furniture". Who is going to improve the level are the coaches and players who arrive and that may add something new. I already have seven years of Premier League. I belong here a little, I am no news."

Even when he was in Chelsea, to coach another club in England was never a problem for Mourinho, as he admitted in an interview to BBC. We don't know if Mourinho was just offering his opinion or if there were already rumours around:

"On the day Mr. Abramovich thinks I am not good enough to work in Chelsea, I will want to keep on working and, if possible, in England. I can see myself coaching another club in England."

For Pep Guardiola this will be a new experience in English lands. Another one! But coaches need these challenges. When he was still coaching Barcelona, and him going to Munich was not expected, he stated that for a manager to grow he needed to coach different players in different contexts. About the players he left in Spain and in Germany he stated that "Any coach depends on his players and the way they play. It is always going to be a big challenge."

Since Txiki Begiristain arrived to Manchester, taking his colleague Pep to the City was only a matter of time. It was speculated that before going to Munich, he could have gone to England. It wasn't then, it will be now! The City provides everything for Guardiola to do what he considers being the most correct for a team that, in spite of the many million, is missing an identity like the neighbour, the United, managed to build under Ferguson.

For starters, he called Arteta, the Spanish player with a great knowledge of the English championship due to his path through Arsenal and Everton. He stated as follows during his presentation:

> "I want to prove myself here, after I have done it in Barcelona and in Bayern. We have to make City play good and that the fans feel proud. We will see which titles we can win, but I want, above all, that we enjoy what we do. For me, that is the most important. But I cannot do it alone: I need the players and all the fans."

Let's wait and see how England is going to welcome the Spanish and rejoice with this relationship between the two best coaches ever. Mourinho is 'getting back' to England for the third time. There was great speculation about the Portuguese going to the Manchester United, but May 24th 2016 ended it all. It won't be like his first arrival to Her Majesty's lands, nor anything like "The ego has landed", a pun with the sentence of the astronaut Neil Armstrong – the eagle has landed on the moon – after Apolo 11 landed for the first time on the moon in July 1969.

At that time, David Moyes, curiously the first manager to fail the attempt of getting someone with a vision to gradually replace Ferguson in the Manchester club, stated "(...) that it isn't possible to show that type arrogance in this country and stay unpunished. I think there are several in line waiting to punch him."

But times have changed. Mourinho is no longer the Special One but the Happy One. Or used to be, let us wait and see what happens in Manchester. Mourinho probably is still an expert in the communication game, anticipating what is needed to condition the other players. Or his own. On the other hand, Mourinho – they already existed of course, but– made these emotional and mental games more visible, but it can be assumed that all other managers, with their different personalities, will be up to the standards of these mental games and profiting from emotions the best way possible!

For the 2016/17 season the victory of a foreigner manager can be foreseen. Even because all candidates are managed by non-British. If we count all the main English championships and the first leagues, the two biggest clubs of the city of Manchester wan 24 titles, 20 for United and 4 for the City. From the 24 seasons of the Premier League (since 1992), 15 champion titles were won by the Manchester teams, 13 for the red devils and 2 for the citizens. In those same championships 10 of the titles were won by non-British managers, 3 by Mourinho when he was in Chelsea.

This said, and history is what it is, especially in a super competitive league, the two Manchester clubs, in theory, will divide the favouritism with Chelsea and Arsenal. Although this last one has been a candidate that when time comes doesn't take the opportunities to become a winner.

However, expectations are increasing. To understand the carte blanche the managers will have in their clubs to change whatever. Mourinho has a quite different philosophy from Van Gaal, as Guardiola has from Pellegrini. This last one even complained that the notice time by his club had been quite wrong. That the players had started to think about the new season too soon. On the other hand, Guardiola stated that he was preparing to move to the City, the club of the mogul Kahldoon al-Mubarak, from Abu Dabi, but even so, he would be able to achieve a good result for his Bayern: "I am like a woman, I know how to think about more than one thing at the same time."

José Mourinho will probably return to his mind games against Guardiola, like he did in Madrid. But the Catalan manager won't be the only target, it is expected that the French Wenger will continue to be one of his favourites, like it has already been several times. Besides, with the Manchester clubs assuming the favouritism together with the Chelsea and the Arsenal, the Portuguese will probably state again that Arsenal's manager is going to be once more the voyeur: "He likes to watch others. There are people who, when at home, have a big telescope to see what's going on in other families."

About the mind games, Mourinho said some time ago that he didn't do them. And that those didn't affect him. Indeed, the Portuguese manager even stated as follows: "There isn't a single comment, a statement of a manager, of an opposing player, that affects me in any way or that changes my way of thinking about anything. On the other hand, I clearly felt that I have changed behaviours with the things I say." It is quite an interesting statement, but probably, when it was said, it had for sure other goal than just approaching the mind games theme, or not.

Guardiola won't probably go in for the kill like Mourinho has done several times. But it is a characteristic that Mourinho allies well with his emotional intelligence, taking advantage of that later on to instigate his opponents even against their future opponents. There will be no chance to state that the Newcastle will park a cow on the pitch and then stop the match because of the cow, since the relegated but there will be other clubs for sure.

Arsene Wenger from Arsenal, one of the direct opponents of the red devils and the citizens, said something about Guardiola kinder than he ever could say about the Portuguese Mourinho: "Barcelona's philosophy is bigger than just winning or losing a championship. Guardiola is one of the representatives of this philosophy and made this philosophy a winner. It is one of the reasons I like him so much." Let's see how it goes now that Guardiola has the chance to take Arsenal away from the title again.

To finalise we recall two episodes. An old one, at the time of the European Super Cup finals between Bayern Munich and Chelsea in Prague, which ended with a victory of the Bavarian, Mourinho let slip the following: "Whenever I play against Pep, I end up with ten men. Must be some UEFA rule." Watching Mourinho has we have been doing, it wouldn't be surprising that at the first expulsion in his United playing against the City, Mourinho would return to those statements. The same won't probably happen with Guardiola in case there are any penalty kicks against the United, after Mourinho once have said that there wouldn't be any penalties against the reds.

The second episode, the words of two iconic players of the United:

> *Eric Cantona on Mourinho going to his United: "I love José Mourinho, but in terms of the type of football he plays I don't think he is Manchester United. I love his personality, I love the passion he has for the game, his humour. He is very intelligent, he demands 100% of his players. And of course he wins things. But I don't think it's the type of football that the fans of Manchester United will love, even if they win. He can win with Manchester United. But do they expect that type of football, even if they win? I don't think so." The French would prefer the choice had been the 'other', Pep Guardiola: "Guardiola was the one to take. He is the spiritual son of Johan Cruyff. I would have loved to have seen Guardiola in Manchester [United]. He is the only one to change Manchester. He is in Manchester, but at the wrong one."*

> *Peter Schmeichel, one day before the contracting of José Mourinho was formally announced, considered José Mourinho to be the only one to turn around Manchester after Van Gaal as head of the United managing team: "On the top of Mourinho's list was always Manchester United. Now they have a guy that is supposed to be the biggest manager in the world, the one that really could save Manchester United", even because "He will be prepared and ready to do it but he has to go back to the values of the football club"*

Scenes of next chapters

"I don't know if I will be able to change you,
but your country is not going to change me.
I am not one of those who lose their identity."

José Mourinho

"I only claim one thing for myself: I love what I do.
And in the end it is all about moments in our careers,
all is heading for those moments when we love
what we do."

Pep Guardiola

This is probably one of the seasons creating more expectations, since we can follow the Premier League at any time. Every year this competition gives us reasons to dream and let ourselves go for a cause, a team, a manager that make us follow the league as our own. We leave behind little things on our daily lives to follow the fight for the title, to see if a player stays or goes.

Everything suggests that this season the fight for the title will have the same players. And natural, taking into account the investment. The teams from Manchester, Chelsea and Arsenal from London, Liverpool and yet another Londoner team, Tottenham, all peeking. All trained by foreigner managers will different profiles, little details that make all the managers of the Premier League actors in a movie every year running for the Oscars of the best competitions.

Like Mourinho stated, "I like this league a lot, this competitiveness, this mentality, these daily difficulties", and we will possibly have a champion different from the one of the previous season and everything suggests the competition will be going on until the final sprint.

We believe that there will also be more communication between the managers than in the former season. Mourinho is synonym of a positive stir. Guardiola will be another target for those who already rule in England, since there are already several kings and potential kings. One of them, the German Klopp, when he played against Pep at the Bundesliga, stated the following about the Spanish manager:

> "He has the incredible ability to develop teams. His game style is too complex, really too complex. It is unique and very hard to fight. He did it in Barcelona and is doing it again in Munich."

Will he be able to do it in the City? Or is it that, like Mourinho says, the Premier is different from La Liga or the Bundesliga? Because in Her Majesty's country the champion is indeed harder to decide than in a championship with three lead players like in Spain, or just one or two like in Germany.

What the Premier League also allows, considering that it is more transparent than other leagues even in the way the managers are exposed in terms of communication, is that we can learn and visualize the behaviours of the managers. Their interactions, the way the press and the media offer true research material.

The leadership of someone over another is a behaviour at the same time natural and not very human. Mourinho says it often in his talks that one of the main roles of a manager is to make someone think about his mate and not himself. Natural behaviours because throughout history we read and learn that the largest territorial conquests were carried out be groups lead by someone. Not very human because the human being has a comfort zone which reinforces and likes us to act only for our own good. And when we have to put ourselves in someone else's shoes, either to better understand those led or the colleague, is something that takes the attention from our inner selves, being us, as humans, primarily selfish beings.

Speaking about groups, we also have several examples of teams, both in sports and other organizations, which having several individuals with high skills and talent for the tasks, fail as a team and sometimes with serious consequences. Talking about the 2015/16 season we understand that teams like Manchester United, Manchester City, Chelsea and Arsenal– just to mention these four – invested millions, which could be the budget of the other 16 teams of the Premier League all together for several seasons.

And here is where our Mourinhos and Guardiolas come in, to work the skills for the tasks and the need of the players to understand and realise that for their performance in that group task, the behaviours and attitudes of the several members have to be interconnected so that they can work in an efficient way.

In companies, the group efficiency is the balance between shared group skills with the individual skills when assigned, coordinated and integrated with the resources for the success of a concerted answer to specific situations. In group sports, like football, there is something else: the opposition of two teams with identical goals, to score and avoid to suffer goals from the opposing team. In this relationship, both teams need to coordinate their players (intra-team coordination) through a group strategy which takes into account the opposition of the other team (inter-team coordination) in an evolving context.

Let us wait for the several excellent managers of this season to captivate us and teach us more about football, leadership, teams, practice, alignment and an endless set of individual and group behaviours. We are also demanding, so we always want the best!

Bibliography

Amieiro, N.; Barreto, R.; Oliveira, B. & Resende, N. (2006). Mourinho, Porquê tantas vitórias. Lisboa. Gradiva.

Balague, G. (2012). Pep Guardiola – another way of winning. London. Orion Books.

Barclay, P. (2006). Mourinho – autonomia de um vencedor. Lisboa. Público.

Blanchard, K. (2003). Bom trabalho. Cascais. Pergaminho.

Cubeiro, J. C. & Gallardo, L. (2011). Mourinho vs Guardiola. Lisboa. Prime Books.

Cubeiro, J. C. & Gallardo, L. (2012) Código Mourinho – decifrar o êxito do Special One. Lisboa. Planeta.

Cubeiro, J. C. (2010). Aprender del 'coach' Guardiola. Harvard Deusto Business Review. Ediciones Deusto Junho.

Damásio, A. (2010). O livro da consciência. Lisboa. Círculo de Leitores.

Eccles, D. W. & Tenenbaum, G. (2004). Why as expert team is more than a team of experts: a social-cognitive conceptualization of team coordination and communication i sport. *Journal of Soprt & Exercise Psychology, 26*, 542-560.

Ferguson, A. (2014). Alex Ferguson, a minha autobiografia. Lisboa. Casa das Letras.

Hodge, K., Henry, G., & Smith, W. (2014). A case study of excellence in elite sport: motivational climate in a world champion team. *The Sport Psychologist*, 28, 60-74.

Katzenbach, J.R. & Smith, D.K. (2001). Equipes de alta performance. Rio de Janeiro. Editora Campus.

Lança, R. (2012). Como formar equipas de elevado desempenho. Lisboa. Escolar Editora.

Lança, R. (2014). Coach to Coach. Lisboa. Prime Books.

Lança, R. & Lopes, M. (2015). Controlled autonomy and autonomous control: A model of coach-athlete relationship. *Journal of Sport Pedagogy and Research, 1(8)*, 102-109.

Lourenço, L. (2010). Mourinho, descoberta guiada – 5ª edição. Lisboa. Prime Books.

Luz, N. & Pereira, L. M. (2011). Mourinho, nos bastidores das vitórias. Lisboa. Prime Books.

Perarnau, M. (2014). Pep Confidential. Arena Sport. Edinburgh.

Pina e Cunha, M. & Rego, A. (2013). Super Equipas. Lisboa. Actual.

Rapaport, R. (1993). To build a winning team: na interview with head coach Bill Walsh. *Havard Business Review, Jan-Fev*, 111-120.

Sérgio, M. (2009). Filosofia do Futebol. Lisboa. Prime Books.

Sitkin, S. & Hackman, J. (2011). Developing Team Leadership: An Interview With Coach Mike Krzyzewski. *Academy of Management Learning & Education, 10*, 494-501.

Soriano, F. (2009). A bola não entra por acaso. Lisboa. Gestão Plus.

Ulrich, D & Smallwood, N. (2012). "What is talent?". *Leader to Leader, 63*, 55-61.

Several news taken from Portuguese and International press.